& SELF IMPROVEMENT

MY JOURNEY TO ACCEPT PLANET EARTH

ERIC Y. CHEN
http://iautistic.com

Copyright © 2007 by Chen Yixiong, Eric
ISBN: 978-981-05-8937-0
Revision 2.3 – 1st Printing – Sep 07
Printed and Bound in Singapore by Kentrich Trade Press

Disclaimer: This work is not a substitute for medical or professional advice. Please consult a qualified professional if you require such advice.

TABLE OF CONTENTS

C1: PREFACE

I am Eric Chen, a 24 year old with a diagnosis of Autism Spectrum Disorder. I decided to change my life a few years ago. Instead of dismissing emotions as irrational, I chose to experience them as deeply as possible. Instead of treating humans as alien life forms, I chose to accept my identity as a human being and experience my human life. As I explored my inner world, I slowly awakening to the instincts that autism suppressed in me.

My perception of the outside world solidified from a flat video screen into 3-dimensional reality. I developed an instinctive sense of inappropriate verses appropriate words and actions that guided me in my social interactions. My mind cleared up and I could make decisions without the panic that used to overwhelm me. Instead of finding bodily contact disgusting, I developed the desire for intimacy and can now choose to use it to enhance my social experiences. Most importantly, I found myself developing a sense of kinship and bonding. I became concerned for my new friends and my family members.

Seeing that I had stepped beyond autism's limitations, I wanted to share my experiences and the subtle features of the autistic consciousness I experienced. This was not an easy choice. I knew that without funding and support from professionals and organizations, I had to do my work alone. Without guidance from other people, I had to find my own way. I knew that other people might discriminate against me when I seek employment. I knew that there was no guarantee that people will accept my work or find it of value. Very importantly, I had to defy my mother's wishes. Instead of taking a well-paying computer job, I chose to make the world a better place by sharing about autism.

Undeterred by the lack of support and various failures, I published 2 autism books, made my autism website, created my original autism materials and stepped into a new life in a foreign land that I have never seen before. After many sacrifices and struggles, I present with this book, the insights that I had won with my sweat and tears. May it inspire the world!

C2: INTRODUCTION

I come from a poor family in Singapore, which struggled to make ends meet. As I grew up, my mother realized that something was wrong with me. I did not look at her when she spoke. I tended to repeat her words or give irrelevant answers. I ignored her and sat alone by myself reading books.

The family doctor was unaware of autism and said that I would outgrow these behaviors. My mother thought that I merely had some communication difficulty, but she could not afford to send me to a speech therapist. She did not have an English education that would have given her access to professional help. However, she loved me and spent whatever little money she had to buy me good food, nursery song cassettes and hire a private English tutor.

In kindergarten, she home-schooled me when I missed lessons due to asthma attacks. In Primary school, she tried to stop the bullying I received, and helped me clear up some misunderstandings with a teacher. With her help, I eventually graduated with a Diploma in Logistics from the mainstream educational system. However, while my mother could help me from the outside, she could not see my inner experiences. Not knowing about autism, she often held me up to the standards of my non-autistic peers. I was found wanting - too slow, too clumsy, too gullible and too unwilling to change my ways.

I broke things. I could not sense the meaning in her verbal instructions and needed her to repeat a few times. I shared inappropriate information with other people. I did not make friends and play with other children. I could not tell her about what happened to me. When I went to the doctor, she had to explain my syndromes and medical issues for me.

Yet, how could I explain something that I was not aware? How could I change the behavior that I did not know was under my control? How can I do something that I could not understand? Fortunately, now I have the capacity to become aware of my experiences. With this, I do my best to paint the ineffable experiences I had into words. If only my mother had read this book 2 decades ago...

C3: ABOUT AUTISM

Since most readers have already heard of the typical explanations on autism, I am using a different, more imaginative approach to explain this topic.

Imagine a world whose inhabitants consist of pure energy that live without physical bodies. They have no need for speech because they understand each other telepathically. They do not have faces, but identify themselves with unique data codes. They do not feel emotions, for it is alien to their design.

Because of their telepathic links, their experience of individuality is more of a collective unity rather than separate selves. Their minds merge in and out of each other like clouds, giving them instant empathy with each other. Hence, they have no conflicts or misunderstandings. However, they remain separated by preferences of what they would like to experience and different opinions on how to achieve goals and interpret data.

With their advanced technology, they have no survival needs and have nothing left to explore in their physical universe. To pass their time, they explore the mental realm of knowledge, create artificial simulated worlds and occasionally construct new inventions. They live in giant Dyson spheres, absorbing energy from their host star. No longer needing bodies, they live as program codes in a supercomputer facility of unthinkable complexity and intelligence. In terms of intelligence, they are to humans what humans are to viruses. Human beings could hardly hope to understand them.

What if one of these computer beings visited planet Earth and became a human being? What kinds of struggles would that this person experience? What syndromes would this person exhibit? What would this person feel?

What if there are many worlds like this, each hosting different peoples. What if some have emotions, but of a variety alien to humans? What if some have bodies, but of a very non-human kind? What if some of them have different senses that work differently from the five physical human senses? What if some of them came from worlds with different laws of physics, such as those allowing magical powers? We can let our imagination run wild contemplating the infinite possible worlds and the challenges their inhabitants face as they come to Planet Earth and live human lives.

While I do not claim that the above descriptions are literally true, I use them as a helpful metaphor to understand autistics as "Foreign Tourists" rather than as psychiatric patients. Simplifying the metaphor, we can imagine the autistic as a new arrival from an imaginary place with the following features:

1. **Complete**: Nothing is missing or inadequate.
   a. There is no lack, thus no need to do anything.
   b. There is no need to do anything, thus no choice.
   c. There is no choice, thus no individuality.
   d. There is no individuality, thus everyone is equal and similar.
2. **Perfect**: Everything is all at once whole and beautiful.
   a. Change is not possible, so there is no Time.
   b. Without change, there is no comparison.
   c. Without comparison, there is no criticism or praise.
3. **Unlimited**: Nothing is impossible.
   a. There are no limits, so no boundaries.
   b. There are no boundaries, so no space or movement.
   c. One's consciousness is dispersed, not confined to a body.

As autistics are adapted more for this foreign land, they need Tour Guides to explain Life on Planet Earth and to help them activate their instincts. Many textbooks define autism with 3 characteristics: communicating difficulties, social interaction problems and rigid thinking. I believe that autism is more complex. I define autism as an instinctive impairment that includes (1) time, (2) space, (3) Self, (4) Emotional Awareness and (5) Senses.

Time

Time: Without temporal instincts, the human experience of time such as flow, perception and complexity become unsolvable puzzles. Bad planning abilities (arising from a poor understanding of cause and effect) and rigid habits (arising from fear of the future) are some of problems I encountered.

1. **Intention**: I could not feel or see the big picture. I did not know how to set intentions so that my body and mind can improvise the required action to achieve my goals. Thus, I could not "get to the point" or understand "the point" that others conveyed.

2. **Causality**: I was unaware of cause and effect arising from people, although I may understand very well cause and effect arising from inanimate objects in a static system. While I had the logical-computer model, I lacked the human intention-emotion model. Thus, I disliked unexpected changes and involving people in my work as it made the future unpredictable.

3. **Consequences**: I was not aware of the consequences that I will encounter with my choices. As I could not see or feel how I could create my own future, I over-simplify and misrepresent situations, become over-confident and arrogant. Sometimes, I made rash, ill-advised decisions.

4. **Constancy**: My perception of time may slow down or speed up, as my internal awareness clock was not "tuned in" to my body's timekeeper. This may cause excruciating anxiety (when sped up) and extreme boredom (when slowed down).

Space

Body: I did not know that I had a body and that I lived in a 3-dimensional world. I could not instinctively sense how the laws of physics act on objects in the world around me.

1. **Space**: Lacking the physics instinct, I saw everything flat as if like a TV set. My imagination was devoid of mass, structure, texture and location. I could not intuitively predict the expected behavior of physical objects. Thus, I was very clumsy and accident-prone.

2. **Location**: I was unable to determine the location of my body parts by instinct. I had to find and lock onto them with my eyes.

3. **Maintenance**: As I neither deprive joy nor feel the urge to take care of my body, I neglected it. Without feedback from my body, I could not feel the warning signs of diseases or the need for good personal hygiene.

(Human) Self

Relationship: As I did not know how to relate based on individuality and emotions, I ignored both and tried to be as objective as possible. Unable to feel the emotional overtures in relationships, I mistook transactional relationships for real friendships.

1. **Self-Definition**: Every one of us will have to make difficult and painful choices sometime in our life. The choices define "Who We Are". Instead of choosing with conscious reflection, I used to make choices by logic, obedience or unthinking avoidance. Thus, I did not understand self-definition, which is the core of individuality. Without grasping the concept of individuality, I also failed to understand human relationships.

2. **Human Design**: We create objects for each other's use. We communicate in a way that our target audience understands. We arrange our lives so that we can also facilitate the lives of others around us. I failed to understand this concept of "human facilitation" via "human design", thus my actions and speech were often irrelevant or inappropriate.

3. **Reciprocation**: A sustainable human relationship requires a give and take. We have a desire to share with each other as well as an instinct for detecting "cheaters" who take from us without sharing in return. Without this dance of give and take, it is difficult to sustain any relationship. I could only create intermittent and unstable relationships with other people because I failed to use and facilitate reciprocation.

Communication: I thought of communication as a form of information transmission or debate. I did not understand the need for and limitations of communicating with others. Although my logic might deduce otherwise, my subconscious mind assumed that all beings are telepathic and homogeneous. Thus, their preferences and perspectives were similar to mine. I liken the disagreement between logic and intuition to emotional carsickness. Logically, I could accept other's behaviors. Emotionally, I felt upset and agitated that they defied my intuitive model.

1. **Cohesion**: People communicate to create group cohesion by maintaining the mood and opinion of their group to agree with each other. Although individuals have different opinions, they cover these up by agreeing on the fundamental principles behind these opinions. Such agreements reinforce the sense of being in the "same tribe", making people likeable and trusting of each other. Thus, they can find joy in each other's company. Because I did not understand this, the people around me do not accept me into their social groups.

2. **Influence**: People communicate to influence each other, such as by stating words in a certain way to persuade other people to make a certain decision. Mutual Influence is an important mechanism to create cohesion, because if people do not accommodate with each other, human society would be impossible to maintain. Unfortunately, because I did not know how to create and exercise influence, I created unnecessary obstacles and misunderstandings in my life.

3. **Holism**: Communication does not consist of words alone, but also body language, speech tone and intentional actions. Instincts guide people to express their emotions and intentions through these non-verbal channels without conscious thought. Communication arises as an impression-experience, where the content lies with the emotional feeling of the experience, not the actual words conveyed. If the instincts for emotional awareness and intentions fail, then the dependent instinct of reading body language also fail, creating a social handicap.

Imagination: Although I started with only the understanding of concrete, logical and literal objects, it did not stop me from developing a rich imagination consisting solely of events and inanimate objects. However, because I could not imagine people, I could not relate to them in reality.

1. **Pretense**: I could understand the concept of using symbols to represent an object and could pretend to be an inanimate object such as a train by imitating its behavior and sound. However, not understanding intentions, separate bodily experiences and other aspects of self-hood meant that I could not replicate imaginary selves into dolls, storybook characters or other people. Thus, I gained little wisdom about other selves from reading stories or acting.

2. **Lying**: It takes effort to create and remember a fictitious situation that other people will believe. Due to my lack of instinct for simulating the thought and emotional reactions of other people, I found it difficult to lie successfully.

3. **Human Design**: Most people are more interested in the usefulness and functionality of an idea or creation because this feels more meaningful to them. Because I was blind to "Human Design", I was disrespectful of practicality and chose to focus on beauty or perfection instead.

(Human) Emotional Awareness

Meaning: The perception of meaning is not a mental judgment but an emotional realization. It comes as a unified meaningful experience, not as a dictionary definition. However, my understanding stood separately from my body, will and emotions. With only logic to guide me, I mistook the symbol for the object and the map for the territory. While I superficially seemed very knowledgeable, I could not apply what I know to solve my problems or to understand people.

1. **Detached**: I had a fragmented awareness and was not aware of my body, emotions, thoughts and intentions. Thus, I felt like a detached observer rather than a living participant. As I did not own any of my experiences and thoughts, my memories, facts and thoughts exist in chaos without any coherent sense.

2. **Unaware**: Until Secondary school, I did not know that I existed. My awareness was of low quality much like intermittent sleepwalking. My choices tend to arise from avoidance of negative stimuli and obedience of instructions issued by other people.

3. **Purpose**: I did not belong here on Planet Earth. I could not feel the warmth of human relationships. Living in a hopeless vacuum, I clung to my only source of delight and meaning: my inner mind where I made exciting discoveries and new inventions. I was obsessed with collecting and classifying knowledge of interest because they build a rudimentary sense of self. "I" expand the more "I" eat such food for thought.

(Human) Senses

Senses: My mind distorted the experience of my senses, making it difficult for me to experience them in a meaningful way. The distortions are usually subtle but serious enough to affect the way I live.

1. **Integration**: Sometimes I was not aware of what people were saying, although I had sensitive hearing. Like hearing a familiar but unintelligible foreign language, their words entered my mind but did not register as meaning. Other people often thought that I was not paying attention.

2. **Detachment**: I could only feel a very mild and detached version of sensory pleasures. However, this detachment only moderately dulls negative emotional and sensory experiences. Starved of pleasure, only anxiety and pain existed in my world. I can relate to why some autistics try to commit suicide.

3. **Coordination**: I found it difficult to coordinate my actions, decision making and sensory input in real time because these systems do not interconnect properly with each other. I need much time to process my sensory data and required actions manually. Being a cashier was one of the most stressful experiences in my life.

4. **Filtering**: I found it hard to focus when noise was present. As my family has a habit of leaving the television on and playing loud music, I resorted to listening to calming music, wearing earphones and working late into the night.

Common Misunderstandings of non-autistics

1. **"You must learn to put yourself in others' shoes"** – This classical statement irritates many autistics. They have already tried their best and do not feel that it is fair for them to carry the burden of constantly compromising with other people.

2. **"Hurry up"** – Without the benefit of temporal and causality instincts, an autistic needs more time to work out what to do. Hurrying him will only lead to impulsive actions or decisions, which we may come to regret later.

3. **"You must learn to socialize and be with other people"** – Without the ability to enjoy social gatherings and lacking the instinctive skills to do so, the autistic often finds no meaning in socializing. I suggest sparing him the agony.

4. **"This is simply the way things are"** – Many non-autistics tend to dismiss the autistic's questions as common sense and refuse to explain using a logically convincing way. The autistic may react to this disrespect by stubbornly refusing to cooperate. Very soon, the pot will be calling the kettle black.

5. **"You are wrong"** – This is the beginning of either a long debate or temper tantrum. Be wise and patient: Explain the situation step by step. For those who are unable to do so, it is best to let someone else handle it.

What non-autistics can do to help

An autistic may not even be aware of his social situation and does not have the benefit of his instincts to guide him. Here are some guidelines:

1. **Leave him alone if he is angry** - He will not listen anyway. Approach him when he is in a better mood.

2. **Never nag an autistic** - He hates it. Since he may find it very difficult to win verbal arguments, he may agree just to stop the verbal torture. However, he will still be angry and dissatisfied, which may cause temper tantrums or sabotage later.

3. **Be gentle and patient** - Avoid blame. When he behaves inappropriately, it is often better to tell him the appropriate action

first, and then explain why step by step. He needs time to reflect and write down his thoughts.

4. **Find a confidant for him** - He prefers an intense, quality relationship with one person, not having 100 friends. This person must be accommodating, patient, wise and genuinely interested to help him. Unfortunately, parents may be unsuitable for this role as he may have erected psychological defenses against them.

5. **Give yourself a break** – If you are working with an autistic for a long time, you will need to rest. Otherwise, you may lose patience.

Common Misunderstandings of Autistics

1. **"Life is a meaningless struggle"** – It is unfortunate that we may have yet developed our instincts to allow us to experience the social dimension of human life with ease. If we do so, life can be fun and meaningful.

2. **"Non-autistics always lie"** – It is unfortunate that most non-autistics could not provide a satisfactorily verbal answer of why they always distort the truth. It is also unfortunate that we tend to have only room for one version of the truth, and that we do not perceive and feel the group dynamics that go beyond truth and lies.

3. **"Social Rituals are totally unnecessary"** – It is unfortunate that non-autistics do not explain and document their culture in a way that we can understand. Much of what they do makes perfect sense if we experience the emotions and social instincts that they feel. The fact that we are blind to their situation does not mean that we are right in this view.

4. **"I am always compromising"** – It is unfortunate that we are often blind to the effort and compromises that other people have made for us, because our instincts for causality and reciprocation are impaired. If we were to grasp that, perhaps we will feel so guilty that we instantly "compromise".

5. **"I am always discriminated"** – While it is true that many people discriminate against autistics, they do not do always it with malice. The feeling is likely to be mutual: until autistics change your mind about other people, these people will probably not change theirs.

6. **"I can understand non-autistics by watching TV and reading books"** – Non-autistic advice often mislead autistics, who lacking the instincts and frame of mind to interpret them. This tempting thought creates "false confidence", making autistics believe that they can do something even if they are incapable of doing so. The resulting unshakable confidence seems like arrogance to other people.

What autistics can do to help

Non-autistics may be mysterious, but they are not necessarily malicious. As it takes two hands to clap, if you take the effort to understand them, you will see the kinder and gentler side of them:

1. **Focus on Intention, Ignore Mistakes** – Unless we are in a debate or court of law, we can ignore the non-autistic's imprecise language and inaccurate facts. Instead, focus on the intention of the speaker. Communicate with them based on their intentions, not mistakes.

2. **Show Respect** – Non-autistics function in a hierarchical system, and you are more likely to be at the bottom of the hierarchy than at the top. In this case, make sure you know where you stand and show the respect due to them. Even if you are higher in hierarchy, it will benefit you to respect those subordinate to you.

3. **Show Effort** – No matter how hardworking you are, it is useless if other people do not know of your effort. Show your effort by keeping them occasionally informed of your difficulties and working conditions in the least obstructive way possible (e.g. sending an email just before you leave if you are working late).

4. **Reciprocate, but not rigidly** – When people do you a favor, social rules dictate that you help them back. This is the human instinct to help each other. Give them their due, or at least the impression of appreciation.

5. **Express your Highest truth** – Tell the truth, but put the emphasis on the positive that both parties can mutually agree with. Discuss the negative if you must, but always leave room for it to turn into the positive.

C4: SCHOOL LIFE

I went to school because my mother commanded me to do so. I was quiet and did not have behavioral problems like throwing tantrums. "*A soft-spoken and diligent pupil*," wrote my Primary 3 teacher in my report book. My Primary 4 teacher wrote, "*Too quiet in class. Should participate more in class discussions.*" Something interested must have happened afterwards for my Primary 5 teacher to write, "*Eric is a willing contributor to class discussions but needs to apply himself more in his studies.*"

Until Primary 3, my mother visited me in school during breaks to bring me food and protect me from bullies. When she was absent, I hid myself in quiet places so that the bullies could not find me. I held no grudges because I perceived bullying as merely something unpleasant. The idea that people could target "me" was beyond my comprehension.

I focused on studying because I did not know what else to do with my life. As a result, I scored good grades. However, after I awakened to my self-awareness, I found the school an oppressive place where my intellectual abilities were stifled and newly awakened creativity discouraged except in limited areas such as essay writing. Why should I have to study a subject that only seemed like a waste of time to me? Why should I have to solve questions in the manner prescribed in the textbook? Why must I answer the test papers using only the limited and outdated information in the textbook instead of the latest scientific advances that I have just read?

In Secondary 3, I went to see the school principal and requested to switch from the Humanities stream to the Science stream because I knew that I would excel there. I scored A's for science but only C's and D's for history and literature. She was hesitant, claiming that the school had not monitored my performance before. I told her that my science results were consistently excellent. She refused to consider that point as relevant. I braced myself and made a big bet with her, "*Ask me any science question now. If I cannot answer at least 80% of them correctly, I will give up on my request voluntarily.*" She flatly refused to take on this challenge, replying that once she has made up her mind, she will not budge.

With much anger, I stormed out of her office. Since the school was not going to educate me the way I wanted, I vowed to take charge of my education myself. I did take my revenge eventually. Seeing my poor academic results, one of my teachers told me not to take the "A" math exam as it would pull down the school ranking. I purposely took it and flunked. In order to punish the educational system, I refused to study and failed most subjects in my preliminary 'O' level examinations. I would have done the same for the real exams if not because I suddenly developed an unquestioning, irresistible urge to study. For 2 weeks, I rushed day and night to absorb what I refused to touch for more than a year. It worked and I received a decent score.

Feeling that the educational system has betrayed me, I was prepared to go to work straight away after my 'O' level examinations. My mother intervened and insisted that I must study in the Polytechnic (to obtain a diploma). After a short argument, I resigned myself to follow her recommendation. I rationalized it as paying her a debt of gratitude for taking care of me for so long. On hindsight, this was a good choice because it allowed me more time to develop my creativity and intellect while gaining me an important formal qualification if I ever needed to find a job.

Feeling that no one has heard my voice, I wrote a lengthy article entitled "My Opinion on the Problems of the Singapore Education System". Listing out every significant flaw I found, it was supposed to be the definitive guide to my grievances. Unfortunately, except for a reply acknowledging and thanking me for my feedback, I heard nothing more from the Singapore Government.

All this time, my anger drove and motivated me to provide my own education, where I read many books relating to science, psychology, education and business. My life as an individual with free will only began after I rebelled and started making my own choices for myself.

Main Issues

Ignorant of social situations & relationships

Blind to the emotional aspects of human relationships, I understood relationships as transactional exchanges. If someone lent me an eraser or helped me perform a task, I consider him as my "friend". If not, then I lump him together with everyone else as "neutral". Those who bully me or put me in unpleasant situations are lumped as "avoidances". After I developed critical thinking, I also included those who share thoughts, ideas and opinions with me as friends. I never felt the emotions behind friendships until after the Singapore Army drafted me.

Cannot "hear" teacher's instructions

The speech uttered by people often did not register in my mind, although I heard their voices loud and clear. This presented a common problem because the teachers often issue verbal instructions like "bring your paintbrush for art lesson tomorrow". Initially, my mother helped me ask other parents about what happened in class. As I grew up, I learnt to ask a few selected friends by myself over the phone.

In Secondary school, I found a combination of writing down instructions as soon as I hear them, and then checking the list with friends immediately after the lesson eliminates most of my problems. For the remaining problems, I followed my classmates' strategies: copy homework from other classmates, run back home to bring the missing item or buy new items to replace the old ones. Sometimes, I pretended to go to the washroom so that I could secretly visit the school bookshop to buy an exercise book, mathematical compass or art materials needed for the next lesson.

My mother often scolded me for my "inattention". "*At work, your boss will only say his instructions once. If you keep asking him to repeat himself, you can expect to be fired.*" Unfortunately, I did not know how to implement my mother's instruction.

Cannot recognize people

I found it difficult to distinguish human faces. It was like trying to tell two sheep of the same species, color and size apart. Without unusual hairstyles or facial features, the only way to remember is repeated exposure – seeing my classmates in the same classroom for at least 3 weeks. I was hopeless with names (and am still today unless that person interacted with me for quite a while or made a great emotional impact on me).

Over time, I covered up my handicap by using a speaking style that did not require me to know the identity of the person. I replaced names with generic substitutes like titles (e.g. the tuition teacher) or pointing to the person I am referring to and saying "*I was just talking to her and this idea came to me*".

To make the pretense complete, I pretended to know who called me and used a friendly tone over the phone. When people waved to me, I waved back regardless of whether I recognized them or not. There was a humorous incident in the Polytechnic when I thought that a group of people was waving towards me when their target is a teenager behind me. I waved back, and realizing my mistake, pretended to laugh it off as a joke.

In Secondary 3, a classmate caught on to my handicap and asked me to name each classmate in sequence based on his or her seat position. I was unable to give the names of ¾ of my classmates even though I can recognize their faces easily (after repeated exposure).

This handicap had other consequences too. In the confusion of trying to escape or hide during bullying incidents, I could not focus well enough to recognize the culprits or remember what they did to me. Often, I dared not tell my mother that someone bullied me because I needed to indict the bullies in front of the teacher, a task that I was not confident of doing. There was at least one incident where a classmate claimed that I falsely accused him. I did not press charges. If only I could memorize photos of people with their names and general background before every social event...

Today, I feel that each face has an emotional signature associated with it. This emotional landscape and impression identifies each face in an inner database (that is not associated with their names). My perception also highlighted the most unusual features of the face, assisting me further in recognizing it. I still have trouble, but my score is improving.

Cannot connect feedback to reality
I had a mind similar to a blank slate, whose only intention is to collect information and obey instructions. However, my limited consciousness severely filtered my understanding. I can work with real objects that I could see and touch. However, I could not understand words relating to bodily control, as I was unaware that I had a body. Neither could I use my emotions to help me grasp words that referred to something intangible.

Only after I recovered my instincts did I realize that every word contains a "complete concept" of an object including emotional feel, past experiences and a special "knowing" which is beyond words.

In Primary school, I had a brief stint in the choir before the organizers expelled me. I was puzzled about why it happened. On hindsight, I did not realize the instruction "*move your mouth when you speak*" referred to using a certain part of my body in a certain way. Unfortunately, no one physically moved my mouth to explain this to me. The choir teacher must have thought that I never sang.

In Secondary school, I thought that my composition marks depended on luck. I would look at a paper that I barely passed and thought, "*Better luck next time*". I did not realize that the teachers have written certain remarks on my paper for my benefit. Fortunately, I could answer written comprehension test passages with ease by working out the rules of grammar on how to extract the relevant information from the text. As I scored rather well, no one suspected that I did not understand what I have read.

Cannot advocate for myself
When other people misunderstood or wrongly accused me of something, I did not challenge them. I wished that I had a lawyer to explain my case

for me because I needed time to think and put forward an explanation of what happened and how I was involved. Even if I understood the situation, I was often too surprised or shocked to defend myself.

In Primary 5, I developed a big misunderstanding with a teacher who thought that I was bad-mouthing her whenever she punished me. My teeth were chattering because of anxiety, not insults. Fortunately, my mother met her to explain my communication handicap. Afterwards, the teacher became very concerned for me and looked out for my welfare in whatever I did.

Few emotional expressions
While I may have felt very anxious, angry or embarrassed, these emotions often did not show up on my face. No one knew that I had a bad day escaping from bullies and handling unpleasant situations. Sometimes, I may force myself to react, such as swearing in chemical formulas while chasing bullies who ran away with my pencil box.

I often felt emotionless. The frustration that I might have felt during bullying and the anxiety of facing new situations disappeared into an empty void outside my consciousness. However, after enough of my emotions accumulated, a major emotional incident could trigger sulking or crying.

In Primary school, I missed the chance to represent my school for a science competition because another classmate scored a few marks more than I did in a science test. I was eagerly looking forward to this chance of showing off my skills, and I thought that my superior science knowledge would guarantee me my representation. After school, I ran home, told my mother and cried.

History repeated itself in Secondary 4. During my rebellion against the educational system, I completely neglected my studies. When the much-anticipated computer programming competition came, the computer teacher decided that I should focus on my studies and refused to let me participate. Having studied programming 2 years earlier than the other candidates, I thought that my talent would guarantee me that chance. I cried, this time alone by myself.

From secondary school until my Army days, I had "tear attacks" at night a few times per year. I would suddenly wake up for no reason, then a great sadness would well up and tears began to flow. After a few minutes, the sadness ebbed and I could continue sleeping. I did not understand what happened and considered these incidents as minor annoyances.

Different learning style

I liken the classroom to a bus. The students are the passengers, the teacher is the driver and the textbook is the route through knowledge that the class learns. The teacher is in charge of driving the bus. The passengers only need to sit through the journey, taking photographs and notes as they travel. At the bus terminal, they answer some questions to prove that they were paying attention to the scenery. I went with the bus until secondary school, after which I developed a learning style more like a taxi. I went where I fancied, regardless of what the class is doing. I liked to make up my own way of doing things, and solve my problems with my own solutions.

The strange thing is that my understanding is either quite complete or highly incomplete. Until I knew enough parts to see the big picture, I could not easily master a subject. However, once I saw through the system of how something works, I could go from being an idiot to a genius very fast. One example is how I learnt computers.

In 1994, my mother had the foresight to see how computers will become important tools, and did her best to make me computer literate. Hearing from her friends that computers are very hard to learn, she sent me for a basic computer course. However, I found the lessons boring and went around moving icons, exploring system settings and looking inside subdirectories. After all, I had already read the lesson notes and knew everything inside-out. My curiosity irked the computer teacher so much that he asked me not to return after I graduated from the second course. I was more than happy to tell my mother about how boring the lessons were and that I preferred not to go. It also helped my mother save some much-needed money.

I was a still computer idiot in Secondary 1. When one of my friends told me over the phone to type "*.*", he told me "*star-dot-star*" instead of "*asterisk-dot-asterisk*". I proceeded to type "*star dot star*" into the computer and received an error message. My friend never figured out why that simple command did not work for me. During that time, my mother persuaded my father to buy me a new computer. That Intel 486 DX-2 66Mhz running on DOS6.22 and Windows 3.11 was a godsend to me. I became engrossed in my private investigation of how it worked. One of them was to mess up the computer and then call the computer shop for help. As the computer was under warranty and the friendly technician in charge was very responsible, he was obliged to entertain me. I made so many calls one of the technicians in the computer shop told me their feet turned jelly whenever they heard my voice.

Unfortunately, some problems were so serious that the technician had to visit my home to fix the computer. That was a great opportunity to watch to fix my screw-up. Feeling uneasy about these fortnightly visits, my mother gave him a token sum of money as "transportation fees" whenever he came. During his last visit, the technician decided that enough was enough: he write-protected and hid the system files so that I could not mess them up again experimenting with exotic memory managers and caching programs. However, I have already figured out that how to bypass this protection a few days ago. I effortlessly regained full control of the system a few minutes after he left.

Soon, the knowledge of how my computer worked hit me as a simple, wordless knowing. After that, I fixed every problem myself. Near the end of Secondary 2, I was flooded with requests for computer help, taking valuable time away from my little hobbies. I had difficulty saying "no" to my persistent friends, until I discovered that most of them would stop pestering me if I charged a small fee.

In Secondary 2, I took a computer-programming course on QBasic meant for Secondary 4 students. I also taught myself how to write scripts for an online chatting program. Strangely, I did not understand the elementary programming concept of "If-Then-Else", but only "If-Then". I still managed to write complex working scripts that slapped people in chat rooms randomly and calculated encryption codes. I found a porn channel to test run it. It was a success.

In the year 2000, I started taking programming seriously after a regular computer client hired me to improve his online course website on a freelance basis. He told me that (1) it was too slow and (2) clients complained that the system kept logging them out while they went for coffee breaks. A previous team of three programmers had just left for an unspecified competitor and he could not find any replacements yet. After some trial and error, I caught on to the new programming language. Looking at the old code, I felt that it flowed like ugly and inelegant lumps. Apparently, my predecessors copied textbook examples without a deep understanding of the programming system. I looked around the programming documentation, the course website and some documents to learn more about the problem.

Closing my eyes, I thought of how the computer system flowed. Diagrams and charts flashed before me, too fast to see anything. Symbols gushed forth. Textures and shapes moved around in the dark ocean of my subconscious. I could feel the computer interacting within itself and with the person accessing the website. The pieces randomly moved around for a few days. Suddenly, many of them came together and I could feel the beauty and perfection of the program code that I will birth. It was an abstract beauty beyond words, beyond three-dimensional space. Yet it was utterly familiar to me.

My fingers quickly typed the commands, jumping from one module to another module. I would finish a few lines here and then jump elsewhere. The program began to take shape as the different half-finished parts slowly came together just like the ideal model I saw within me. As I constructed most of the program, I saw that the code I wrote flowed smoothly and fast unlike the previous ones.

As I worked, I saw problems that my client did not tell me, such as the fact that people were abusing his online course by sharing their accounts with friends. The system I constructed quickly showed me the solution. I created a simple piece of code that rendered such abuse impossible. I named that code the "rotary door" as the process of logging in would kick any unauthorized user out automatically. I finished my work around 2 to 3 weeks later. My client was pleased to see the waiting time for a page to load had decreased from 8 to ½ a second. In addition, the complaints from users about the system logging them out stopped completely.

Secondary Issues

Bullying
Lacking the protection of a group of friends and behaving so differently from other people, I was an easy target. Unable to appreciate human intentions, I did not realize that bullying included more than physical kicking or shoving. If only I had a lawyer to explain to me the definition of bullying...

1) **Nicknames**: The bullies invented weird nicknames for me. Once, I drew a picture of a finger digging a nose and put a cross on it for a health education project about personal hygienic. They saw it and started calling me "nose-digger". This stuck on me for a few years, until my mother decided to switch me to another school to stop break the cycle of bullying.

In secondary school, I told a shoe shop assistant about the nicknames the bullies used to call me, thinking that it was an interesting topic for discussion. My mother could not stop me as she was in the changing room. The lady smiled nervously and did not reply. After we left, my mother scolded me for talking about embarrassing and inappropriate topics.

I was unable to master nickname calling myself. I had a Secondary school classmate who did not treat me well. His name rhymes with "prison" in Mandarin, so I thought of nicknaming him "prison". My mother was appalled that I had such bad taste.

2) **Losing Verbal Challenges**: One day outside Primary school, I was playing badminton when another child challenged me. [I forgot what he said.] I replied that I would shoot him with bullets from my pistol if he continued. He countered by saying that his laser gun was more than a

match for my pistol. Defeated by my inferior knowledge of sci-fi weapons, I kept quiet.

A bully in Primary school specialized on beating me with words, especially on the school bus. One day after science class, I wondered aloud, "*Since the maggot of fruit files destroy the fruit they are in, would they not do the same if they got into a student's head?*" He seized the chance and said, "*That would be your head that is rotting*". My classmates roared in laughter while I stood dumbfounded.

3) Sabotage: Sometimes the bullies made me do or say things that lead to punishment. My mother once enrolled me for some tuition classes outside Primary school. A cheeky classmate told me to copy him as he pointed the middle finger. Not knowing better, I followed. He then called out to the teacher, "*Look, he is pointing the middle finger!*" Fortunately, the teacher merely told me that it was rude to do that and not to do it again.

Also in Primary school, the bullies tried to trick me into speaking vulgar language. The Mandarin words "*lazy sleep*" and "*chicken white*" (which meant penis and vagina in the Teochew dialect) were especially popular. One of their riddles was, "*Good pig sleeps good sleep, bad pig sleeps bad sleep, lazy pig sleeps in what sleep?*" The other was to tell me to count in Mandarin from 100 to 700 (because it also rhymes with "*chicken white*" with a tone shift.) Once I pronounced the answer, they burst out laughing and teased me for speaking "bad words". This confused me. Eventually, I decided that it was bad to answer questions that provoked laughter. Thus, the bullies had to crank their brains to find new ways of tricking me. After I caught on and refused to answer any riddle, they switched to other bullying techniques.

In secondary school, when the entire school was in church for Mass, somebody threw a few things at my back. He must have timed it very well - just as I turned back with my fist raised to warn him to stop, a teacher saw me and thought that I was talking to someone. She made to sit alone in the front row as punishment.

4) Pranks: One day in Primary school, I found that the water in my water bottle had a strange taste and looked cloudy. Puzzled as to why it became so. I brought the bottle of water home to ask my mother. She told me that it was chalk powder from the blackboard!

5) Throwing items around: The bullies took sadistic joy watching me try to retrieve things that they threw. Sometimes, two or more of them will toss my pencil box to each other and watch me try in vain to outrun their tossing game. They only stopped a few minutes later when they became bored. Messing up my belongings was their backup plan if they could not bully me physically, such as if I stood near the discipline headmaster.

6) Poking body with objects: My neighboring classmate for Primary 5 and 6 occasionally rubbed the metal tip of a ballpoint pen in the small gap between our plastic desks. When the tip became searing hot with fiction, he would poke it into my arm. Although the pain irritated me, it caused no physical damage.

7) Giving bad peer feedback: A music teacher in Primary school had an unorthodox method of giving points: she would ask the class, "How many points should I give to this person?" The bullies made it clear that I should fail the subject. Seeing this injustice, I appealed verbally to a few friends who I knew would help me, but they merely smiled and stayed quiet. [Now I know that they were fearful of offending the bullies.] Fortunately, the teacher was sensible enough to ignore peer feedback for my case.

Exclusion from Team Projects

I prided myself on being independent in my project work, because I knew how difficult it is to ask for help and to coordinate with others. By Secondary 3, I had developed extensive general knowledge (especially in science), a good command of formal English, excellent computer skills and a taste for creative design and neat layout. Although I was capable of handling the entire project single-handedly, I was always the last one to find a team. My teammates often ignored my advice, ordering me to work in the manner they liked. Their bad habits included rushing to finish projects at the last minute and wasting much time (and money) chitchatting at fast food restaurants. I found their tendency of writing badly formatted and disorganized passages copied from encyclopedias atrocious and unoriginal. I felt that it was very unfair that I could not create better quality work because they were too stubborn to listen to me and make simple and easy improvements.

For a Business Law module in the Polytechnic, I had to form a 2-person team to complete a report-based project. My partner was supposed to write half the report, but he only submitted a short passage after much delay. I confronted him and demanded that he show up at 1pm at the computer lab in order to finish his part of the project on time. He agreed, but never showed up for hours. I complained to the unsympathetic lecturer, who insisted that I should learn how to settle my own interpersonal problems. "*In the workplace*", she remarked, "*you have no choice who your colleagues are and you must learn to work with them*". I replied that it was impossible to work with someone who is purposely uncooperative. She replied that she would fail both of us if she did not see both our names in the report. As a result, that jerk got an "A" for nothing. [Unfortunately, I did not know about autism yet.]

Clumsy & Slow
My Primary 4 teacher remarked in my report book, "*He is rather slow in his work.*" I needed time to process verbal instructions or to consider the sequence of how to perform a task. Sometimes, a task was simply too difficult for me. Simple tasks like tying knots, handling a pile of paper, pouring water required much effort and patience because I did not know that I had a body or that I lived in three-dimensional space.

The most difficult question for the first paper of the preliminary 'O' level examination was how to tie up the exam papers. I could not thread the thin string through the small hole in the foolscap paper and around itself a few times to make a knot. [At least my shoelaces were much thicker.] The entire school cohort waited 5 minutes for me. Back at home, I thought about how to solve that problem. 10 minutes later, I put two toothpicks together and taped them. Eureka! My new invention allowed me to thread string in record time.

My clumsiness sometimes cost me dearly. I breezed through the English 'O' level exam and triple-checked all my answers with half an hour to spare. Suddenly, I noticed that I had not followed the instructions for the summary question: "*Leave an empty line between every other line, and leave two empty lines between each paragraph*". I rushed to rewrite my answer, finishing it just as the examiner ordered every one to stop writing. Unfortunately, instead of inserting the corrected summary paper, I panicked and discarded both copies. That cost me my chance to study computers in the Polytechnic as the summary paper contained 20% to 25% of all the marks in the paper.

[Note to readers: The educational system did not care that I was talented in computers. Instead, their computer simply awarded those with the best results first priority in their choices. Those with poor results often have little choice but to take courses they have no interest in. I got my 8th choice, logistics.]

This problem continued to trouble me even after I graduated from the Polytechnic. On the day the Army drafted me, I had to perform certain ceremonies with the other enlistees. As I was unsure of what to do, I followed what my neighbors did. This introduced half a second of delay, which the Sergeant Major noticed. "*You!*" he shouted at me from the stage. "*Why are you so slow? If everyone else can get up and sit down on time, why can't you?*" I kept silent. Fortunately, the matter passed without any incident.

Habitual Ways

While I could accept changes with the school timetable, it still took me a lot of effort to figure out how to do everyday things. Hence, I often relied on habits. Recess time was troublesome. I had to finish my food fast and hide before the bullies finish theirs. There were too many types of food for me to select and I disliked wasting my time waiting in queues (as I neither enjoyed good food nor sought companionship).

For the first few days that I encountered a new school setting, I would research the canteen stalls and apply the following criteria: (1) cheap prices, (2) edible food and (3) short queues. The winning stall will get my business as long as I remained in school, unless I happen to see another better competitor. In upper primary and secondary school, it was *fried bee hoon*. In the Polytechnic, it was plain rice with one selection of vegetables and curry soup.

General Coping Strategies

Learnt English by reading
I used to have no idea what to do, so by default I would engage in one of my favorite hobbies or read books. Reading is probably how I picked up much of my English, developing a formal speaking style with many incorrectly pronounced words. I pronounced "*speculate*" as "*spec-tech-culate*" and "*volunteer*" as "*bore-larn-tier*". My classmates laughed at the latter because the first two syllabuses sounded like "no penis" in Teochew.

Unlike many of my Chinese peers who also speak only Mandarin at home, I was stronger in English, not Mandarin. After an autism sharing, a professor from China asked me why I had difficulty with Chinese characters in school. After a minute of reflection, I explained that Chinese characters consisted of complex 2-dimensional forms while English words are of a simpler 1-dimensional form. It took me much less effort to recall and process the simpler forms.

English-Mandarin Dual Selves
When I started speaking more fluently (perhaps in Primary 4), I separated myself into two parts. The more intelligent, verbal and creative part of me became my English Self, which expressed itself in school. The less intelligent, non-verbal and slow reacting part became my Mandarin Self, which expressed itself mostly at home where I communicated with my mother. As a result, I appeared much less intelligent and capable to her.

I soon discovered that my English Self could handle all my communication and social processing needs, with my Mandarin Self acting only as the translator. As a side effect, my Chinese schoolwork developed an English influence, prompting my Chinese teacher to remark that I wrote my Chinese essays as if they were in English. I also tended to stutter in Mandarin because my Mandarin Self could not keep up with the translation demands.

In order to share more effectively with audiences in China, I began to integrate the 2 selves. Although I began to think natively in Mandarin and allowed the Mandarin Self to communicate without translation, it still had much catching up to do before it can match my English Self.

Partial Independence
Although I strove to do my work independent, I was still highly reliant on my mother at home, such as with my art homework. My mother knew that I could not afford to hand in shoddy work caused by my lack of fine motor control and sense of aesthetics. However, her attempts to teach me how to make "decent artwork" and hold paintbrushes properly never worked.

Inventing Solutions
A Secondary School classmate named Kelly always used the phrase "improvise" whenever any difficulty or challenge came before him. I followed his spirit and chose the policy of inventing solutions to solve my problems rather than asking other people for help. Without knowing it, he became my role model.

Watching Japanese Animation
In Secondary school, my sister first introduced me to Japanese animation with the classical "Sailor Moon" series. We moved on to many different titles (and picked up some Japanese too). Despite cultural differences, these gave me an invaluable glimpse of the lives of my peers, which would otherwise have remained a complete mystery to me.

While it was interesting to hear of Japanese schoolgirls discussing romance, I did not take much note of the social elements. I was most keen to analyze how accurately these shows portray science principles. I also liked to imagine different possible scenarios not explored within the story. I could accept the magical and fantasy elements in these shows and designate them as "not real". The new ideas enriched my imagination and inner life.

[Although my mother encouraged me to watch TV soap operas to learn about the real world, I consistently declined her invitation. I did not like to watch stories with real people, especially when the complex social plot, identity of the characters and constantly changing contexts eluded me. Cartoon characters express themselves in a more obvious and simpler manner.]

Coping with "Inattention"

Write It Down
Writing down checklists and upcoming events proved very useful in helping me remember what will happen. I developed a habit of immediately writing everything of importance down to prevent myself from forgetting. Typically, I wrote them all my stuff in the same dairy so that I never missed them.

Bring everything in a big bag
After checking the timetable and my diary, I consolidated all the items that I would theoretically need to bring and packed them into my bag. Unless I have noted down that I could omit something, I brought everything that every lesson might need. I have learnt never to take chances by omitting items. I may not be sure if we need to use the compass during math lesson or the English workbook during English lessons.

Even without all the books and tools, my Primary school bag comes with:
1. 3 small toilet rolls (i.e. rolled up toiler paper for sneezing)
2. 1 large toilet roll (for backup)
3. 1 bottle of medicinal oil (for stomach indigestion)
4. 1 hot water flask (for asthma treatment)
5. Medicine (if needed)
6. Foldable Umbrella
7. 1 pencil box equipped with a complete suite of stationary (including pencils, 2 blue pens, 2 black pens, erasers, staplers, staple refills)

In secondary school, I removed the hot water flask and added:

1. Water Bottle
2. Spare Writing Paper (both lined and unlined)
3. Hole Puncher
4. Math Protractors
5. Scientific Calculator
6. Foldable fan (to cool myself down in hot weather)
7. A pair of spare glasses
8. A few rubber bands
9. Glue (but later I switched to using scotch tape)
10. A small pair of scissors
11. Plastic bags (both big and small varieties)
12. Small Torch Light (for emergency)
13. Magnetic Compass (for finding directions in case I get hot)
14. Binoculars (in case I need to see something far away)
15. 1 to 2 books (outside the syllabus) for reading
16. Public Transport Guide Book
    (after I started to travel to repair computers and "do business")
17. Spare electronic watch (with broken strap)

In the Polytechnic, I threw out the spare watch and protractions, then added:
1. My personal name cards
2. One-Lens Reading Glasses (my invention to prevent lazy eye)
3. Metal String (to tie or repair stuff)
4. Metal Detector
5. Electromagnetic Field Detector (to detect unhealthy magnetic fields)
6. Laser Pointer
7. Measuring Tape
8. Anti-slip pads
9. At least 3 computer diskettes (for copying data)
10. Small penknife
11. Raincoat
12. Mirror
13. Singapore Street Directory
14. Swiss Knife

By now, I have to put my stuff in boxes for convenient packing. When I went to the Army, I decided to revise my "survival pack". I threw out:

1. Metal Detector
2. Electromagnetic Field Detector
3. Computer diskettes (forbidden)
4. Small penknife (forbidden)
5. Scissors (forbidden)
6. Raincoat (my umbrella was good enough)
7. Most of my plastic bags
8. Singapore street directory (unless I need to go places)

Still undeterred, I added:

1. A bottle Citronella Essential oil (to repel mosquitoes)
2. Small Raincoat (for my bag only)

My classmates often teased for carrying my "tortoise shell". However, I was worried of being unprepared for possible scenarios that I imagined (such as medical emergencies and terrorist attacks). Only after I went to Macau did I stop carrying my "emergency survival pack" everywhere with me.

Childhood Hobbies

Just a note: I suspect that if I had computers and the Internet when I was a child, all my hobbies would probably be computer related.

Feeding birds on a path

I found it interesting to see birds feeding and wanted to control their behavior. I went to a small provision shop below my apartment block and took some beans (without payment). I scattered some of them to bait the birds and lined the rest along a trail. My goal was to make the birds to climb the staircase of my apartment block to the fourth floor. Pecking furiously, the birds climbed partway to the second floor. Unfortunately, all of them suddenly flew away because someone was walking down the stairs. Undeterred, I tried again, but they only got to the second floor. On the third attempt, the storeowner caught me and told me not to do it again. I never did.

Playing with ants

I liked watching ants. I would put a pebble or cup in the middle of ant trails, add bits of sand to obstruct ant holes, or use a spade to dig into ant nests (from a safe distance) and see how they react. After I graduated from Secondary school, I was with my best friend in a new park. I spotted a thick cluster of black ants feeding on an abandoned coconut shell. Nearby, a colony of red ants milled around. I wondered out loud what would happen if I moved the coconut shell with all the black ants over to the red ant colony. My friend acted on my thought and I watched with fascination as war broke out. After a few minutes, the red ants triumphed and took over the coconut shell. After many of them had collected on it, I moved them back to the black ant colony for a sequel. I gleefully observed the different combat techniques and capabilities that the black and red ants used.

Jamming Lift Doors

I wondered what would happen if I stopped the lift doors of my apartment block door from closing. I put some junk mail between the doors but they just slid away as the lift moved. After some experimentation, I found that metallic objects (e.g. nails) and tough fruit shells (e.g. watermelon) worked. Unfortunately, some of the lifts in my block and the neighboring block stopped working because I did not remove the objects after the experiment. My mother told me the next day that some inconsiderate person had sabotaged the lifts. Afraid of a scolding, I kept quiet. However, I decided that it was a bad idea and never did it again.

Scary Lift Game

While coming back from Primary school tuition one day, I suddenly decided that the lift door was a scary thing because when it closes something bad would happen. Hence, whenever I was alone and the lift doors opened, I sprinted down the stairs. This irrational belief stayed with me for a few years until I decided that the lift door was not scary anymore.

Water Games

I once built a water rocket with a rubber valve based on a design from a science book. I pumped air into the rocket but it only made a big splash.

Not willing to give up, I moved it to the toilet and pumped a lot of air into the rocket rapidly. It flew about half a meter before dropping.

I had a tuition teacher in Primary school who caned me for every mistake I make in my work. I broke down and cried at home one day after confessing to cheating so that I can get full marks in his test. My mother soon found me a new tuition teacher. However, I was playing around with squirting water from a small bottle one night when I saw him from my balcony (based on the outline of his body). I aimed my little bottle carefully and counted down the estimated time to squirt. I dared not look out of the balcony in case he saw me, but I think he shouted as the water rained on him.

Fire in Tunnels Game
The playground of my childhood had real sand, unlike the plastic playgrounds today. Sandcastles were too boring, so I decided to play with my own invention. Whenever I went to the playground at night, I dug a tunnel under the sand and lighted a fire in it. I experimented and found that a combination of paper and wax candles worked nicely. Unfortunately, if the bullies saw me, they would step on and collapse my tunnel. They usually left me alone later but sometimes they ordered me to leave so that they can take over the playground. I compiled and went home to read books or play with fish.

Wooden Bridge Music
If I did not have the materials for "Fire in Tunnels" or it was too wet to play, I would stand on the wooden suspension bridge in the playground and move my body so that the planks swing or knock against each other. I tried to make as many different sounds as possible by adjusting how I swung.

Hiding Shoes Game
During a parental gathering for my sister's kindergarten class, I became bored drawing lines and writing chemical formulae in the sand (of another playground). As I lacked candles and there was no bridge to make sounds with, I tried a new idea. I took a pair of sandals from the gathering and I buried them in the sand. The victim saw me and tried to talk to me as she uncovered her shoes, but I ran away and hid in the dark kindergarten

classrooms. Although nothing serious happened, I decided that hiding shoes was a bad idea and never did it again.

Playing with cough mucus
In Primary school, I would occasionally cough up some mucus. One day, I was waiting at a clinic and I went to the playground nearby. I coughed up some mucus and spat it over an ant hole to see how the ants reacted. Later, I became bored and took out some cat brand sparklers that my mother gave me. Then I coughed another bit of mucus on the concrete floor, lighted up the sparkler and put it on the mucus to see what happens. The mucus started boiling as the spark moved through it. My mother saw it and said something (I had forgotten) to me. After that, I did not do it again.

Building Lego Sets
My mother bought me some Lego sets. For years, I entertained myself by constructing different objects. I rarely followed the instruction book as I preferred my own designs. These included a very fast electric cart and some weird looking (and often structurally unsound) towers and walls.

Playing with fire
Fascinated by fire, I liked to see what happens when I burn certain objects. Once I started a fire with some paper in a bowl above a TV set covered by a cloth. I then added some strange smelling twigs from a herb. The fire began to crack and emit sparks, causing the cloth to catch fire. My aunt saw this and quickly put out the fire, scolding me as she did so. Too shocked by her reaction, I did not remove a piece of hot ash that flew onto my forehead. [It made a small white patch on my skin for a few weeks.] My mother arrived and scolded me even more severely. I did not understand what happened but I decided that it was bad to light fires at home, so I stuck to my "fire in tunnel" game.

Reading & collecting scientific data
In Primary school, I kept three small notebooks that had red, blue and brown covers. Inside, I wrote all the interesting scientific facts that I read, such as the melting point and atomic number of various elements. One of my classmates (who was in the bullies' gang) "borrowed" the three booklets and did not return them. After a week, my mother intervened

and called his mother. He returned all three notebooks promptly the next day.

"Raining" downstairs
One day, while bathing in the toilet, I observed brown water flowing down the wall when I sprayed the dusty windowsill. As I sprayed more water, I heard some splashes outside. A large amount of water has flowed to the toilet window of my neighbor below. I liked the sight of water flowing down such a distance and poured more water so that it will flow all the way down to the ground floor. I did not realize that the splashing water irritated my neighbors. I played this game a few times but strangely, they never complained.

Collecting Cactus & Exotic dry plants
I developed a temporary fascination with cactus and exotic dry plants. My parents indulged me with a few of them before they completely refused (perhaps because it cost too much). I liked to put the dry plants on different seashells, coral rocks and decorative items to see how they looked. For the cactus, I observed their different features and was delighted to see them flower and bud. I put the buds around the pot and watched them grow.

Electrical Gargets
As my father was an electrician, I developed an interest in electric wiring after he showed me how he worked with his tools. Later I even repaired some appliances by myself. However, sometimes I electrocuted myself after forgetting to switch off the current. Although it happened more than nine times, I only had some minor swelling of my skin. Fortunately, I preferred working with battery circuits instead of mains electricity. After I had a computer, I plugged an AC to DC transformer into the mains. I ran wires to transmit the low voltage current to a switchbox that allowed me to turn on and off the computer speakers, light bulbs, miniature fans etc.

I modified a laser pen to run from normal batteries so that I could use it for a long time. I experimented to see how far the beam went until I needed to use a telescope to search for the beam. During one of my experiments, the beam strayed into the window of an apartment block and surprised someone. As he ran to the window, I hid so that he could not find me.

My father once bought me a pair of walkie-talkies. I tried to use it to talk but its range was too short. Building a large metal antenna protruding out of my father's room did not improve the reception. Hence, I simply left the walkie-talkie on and monitored it for interesting signals.

Playing with Fish

Later on, I became interested in fishes. My father was also keen to keep some fish, so he got a fish tank, some aquatic plants, rocks, sand and various species of fishes. The new aquarium became my focal point. I started reading about fish, spending hours constantly remodeling the aquatic landscape and pestering my father to buy certain interesting fishes for me. I watched intensely as the fishes interacted with each other and ate their food. Wanting to improve the living conditions for my fishes, I asked my father for a more powerful air pump and better filters but he was not willing to pay for them. I decided to make my own air-water mixing system where the air from the air pump and the water from the tank would mix at the right pressure to fill the air tubes with water and air alternately. I extended the length of the air tubes, so that this will give more time for the air to mix with the water.

Some fishes developed big tummies. Suspecting pregnancy, I followed the instructions in my fish book and isolated them in another tank. A few days later, I found many baby fish. Unfortunately, I could not persuade my father to buy certain special fish food for the fry, as the worms were too large for them to eat. When I came back from school one day, I found that my father had emptied all the small fry into the main fish tank, By now, most of the fry were already eaten by the adult fishes. I saved those that hid themselves and put them back in the small tank. I demanded an explanation but my father refused to offer one. Angered, I thought of taking revenge on him. I made an electrocution device but did not really use it on him. Instead, I wrote an essay during tuition class playing out the ideal scenario:

Sneaking into his room while he slept, I placed some alarm clocks set to ring simultaneously in different places to create confusion. I ran live, exposed electric wires around him and install a talking parrot toy underneath his bed. I put some boxes over his bedroom door and closed it carefully. When the alarm clocks rang, he panicked and tried to get out of bed. This caused him to entangle himself with wires, electrocuting him. As he shouted in anger, the talking parrot toy mocked him by echoing his shouting. After he freed himself, he opened the door only to have the boxes rain down on him. All this time, I stood at the front door taunting him. Before he could catch me, I ran and hid according to a special route I had devised so that he could not find me.

Playing with Front Door
When I was home alone, sometimes I tried to ambush my mother. When she opened the door, a chair holding a bunch of toilet rolls would tip, spilling them on the floor. I did not remember my mother scolding me for that prank.

Sports
I began participating in sports after my asthma attacks stopped. While running, I found that I could switch from running forward to running backwards without interrupting my speed. This was a variation of my "walking forward-backward technique", which I devised as I experimented with various walking styles.

When I played badminton, I calculated the trajectory of the shuttlecock as it left my opponent and estimated its probable location. Instinct then kicked in and I would skip, spin, slide and twist. A friend commented that I looked as if I was dancing. I tended to hit the shuttlecock very high to confuse my opponent. Despite my weird style and my lack of depth perception, I usually played quite well. However, I did not give way to weaker opponents, always striking them with my full abilities.

During swimming lessons, I invented my own swimming style, which worked by rotating my two hands rapidly around each other. I called it the "Dog Style" because a friend commented that I looked like a dog swimming when I used it. I also discovered how to switch from one swimming style to another, and to reverse my direction with almost no delay. To stop my swimming goggles from fogging up, I put a little bit of water in and occasionally shook my head (so that the water would clear the fog).

Electromagnetic Field (EMF) Detection
In Secondary school, I read a book warning about the dangers of "Electromagnetic Field Radiation". Keen to protect myself, I purchased the cheapest detector I can find and tested the EMF fields of everything around me. I found that motors, air conditioners and certain computer parts emit strong EMF fields. I went out with the detector and explored my neighborhood, mapping out underground power lines based on their EMF emissions. My fascination continued for a few months before dying out.

Some Notable Incidents

"Stealing" Cactus
I was on my way to visit a friend and saw a beautiful cactus plant. It was so special that I simply had to take it and look at it closely. As I did so, a man exclaimed, "*don't steal my cactus!*" He rushed out of the apartment door. Sensing that something was wrong, I ran up the stairs and looked down. "*Upstairs!*" he shouted to his wife as he saw me. Without thinking, I took the lift to the ground floor and ran for another two blocks. Afterwards, I decided to take a less dangerous route to my friend's home.

Counting over 130 species in garden
When I could not participate in the sports lessons, I would watch butterflies and other insects crawling in the grass field, identify the different species of plants and play with mimosa plants (which close their leaves when something touches them). With such practice, I was fully prepared when the class went on an excursion to the school science garden. We had to count the number of species of plants there. Most classmates counted 20 to 40 species, one found around 70. However, I found over 130 species because I noticed the subtle differences in the leaves of the grass.

Class Duty

I took class duty in Primary school very seriously. I separated the classroom into many zones, and swept the floor zone by zone and ensured that all the dust went into the dustpan. Then I aligned the tables in a perfectly straight line, evenly separated from each other. Because I allowed no deviation, I took an hour to finish what took only a few minutes for my classmates.

The Wednesday Dog

One evening, I went out to take photographs of animals for a science project. I saw a lanky black dog and followed it up the stairs of an apartment. Cornering it, I took aim with my camera. The dog started barking and lurching aggressively at me, but I did realize that it might hurt me. I became fond this photograph and christened it the "Wednesday Dog". I even wrote an essay all about it.

Warm up exercises during speech and drama exam

I became anxious during a speech and drama examination in school. I suddenly thought of how I did warm-up exercises every morning. Spontaneously, I used my hand to hold up one of my legs and twisted the leg I held up a bit. Puzzled by my behavior, the examiner wrote:

1. Avoid moving around when you speak the poem. Correct posture and stance contribute towards successful speaking. So aim towards developing techniques in performance.
2. The shifting of weight from one leg to another was distracting. Work towards a greater sense of performance when speaking from memory.

Fortunately, I passed the examination by just 2 marks.

Apologizing to teachers

After I became disillusioned with the educational system, I disliked the literature teacher for her strict demands on class work. One day, she detained me for extra remedial lessons. I wrote her a note announcing that she has no right to control my education. I could see her face turning very angry. She then scolded me harshly. After that, I asked my friendly English teacher what to do. He told me that if I made teachers angry, then I should apologize. I asked what if it was not my fault. He replied that it does not matter because I should always apologize if I wanted to have good relationships with my teachers. I apologized the next morning. The literature teacher has since forgotten the matter completely.

One day, after I finished the official experiments in the Secondary school science lab, I thought that I could conduct some of my own design. I laced a thin glass stick with various chemicals, one at a time, and put it over the flame. I found it fascinating how different chemicals could affect the flame color. The teacher saw me and intervened. He stood too close to me so I gently pushed his hand away. Ignoring that, he announced that he would ban me from the lab if I did not apologize and stop doing my experiments. I did not like his attitude and just kept quiet. Later, I remembered the incident of the literature teacher and made a logical decision to apologize. The science teacher did not pursue the incident and allowed me into the lab again.

Sliding Water Bottle Cap
I remember in Secondary school during Mandarin lesson, I placed my bottle cap on a small puddle of water on my school desk. The cap slid down the puddle. I moved it up. It slid down again. As I did this repeatedly, it seemed to focus my mind. The teacher noticed me and said something harmless that I have forgotten. After that, I did not do it again.

Expelled from Computer Club
This incident started in Secondary 2, when I went for a programming class meant for Secondary 4 students. The course instructor just returned from the washroom, and he suddenly exclaimed something. I went to look out of curiosity. On his computer was a screensaver scolding vulgarities at a certain teacher. It was password protected and the instructor could not access his computer anymore. Seeing this, I bypassed the password and reset the screensaver not to activate again. Sometime later, I went to tell the teacher who was targeted (and in charge of the computer club) of my discovery. I suggested that one of his students must have done it. He claimed that he knew his students well

and none of them would do so. I went away puzzled because his logic made no sense.

A few months later, I was attending a computer club lesson by the same teacher about a program that I have learnt long ago. Overly bored, I switched to DOS mode and started programming. I was writing a random number generator that could test if we have psychic abilities. The teacher noticed me and asked what I was doing. I told him that I was programming. He asked the classmate sitting next to me, but he claimed to be ignorant. He then told me, "*Your services are no longer needed any more.*" I thought that it was a good idea because I no longer have to attend any more boring computer lessons.

For the computer club activity of that day, we were to use Print Ship Pro to design posters. In this era before JPEG files, the computer graphics were plain and simple. My classmates could only make simple designs with these. However, I discovered a new design strategy that combines many pictures into a single picture, such as putting an apple into a computer monitor screen. As a result, my design surpassed that of my classmates. Reviewing the designs, the teacher asked me if he could use the design. I graciously agreed, and then left that classroom forever. Looking back, I wondered if he did show it to the principal. "*Oh what a creative student you have*", she might have exclaimed. I wonder if the teacher would mention that he just expelled the student for "disobedience".

Internet Search Competition

In 1997, I represented my school in a search engine competition. We were supposed to participate in a team of 3. However, the other students arrived in school wearing street clothes. The computer teacher (not the one who expelled me) told them to go home and change their clothes. However, they did not return. Leaving without them, we reached the competition venue 5 minutes late. When the time was up, I could answer only slightly more than half of the questions. I told the teacher that I may have disappointed her, but she consoled me and said it was OK. To our surprise, we were one of the top four schools nationwide selected to enter the semi-finals.

The teacher selected another two students for the team. I taught them about the basic search engine techniques as we traveled to the venue. After our arrival, one of the panel officers jokingly said that he would hire me if I made it into the finals. My team was now up against the students of a prestigious school, with many people monitoring our progress live on a big screen behind us. It was the first time I experienced so much attention and so much pressure to perform. The other team beat us. After the competition, the officer told us that while my team found the answers first, we scrolled too fast and missed it. In theory, we would have beaten the other team by a good margin. I felt some regret but was relived that everything was over.

Discovered confidential school report in Recycling Bin

I was walking to the Staff Room, when a special report in the Recycling Bin caught my eye. I took it and found that it was minutes to a meeting about handling disciplinary problems. Some of the points mentioned went against my educational beliefs. I shared it with one of my classmates who also criticized it. After class, I asked one of my teachers why the school had such policies. He was stunned that I had the report and asked me how I got it. I told him. Without any explanation, he confiscated the report. Ever since then, the teachers were wary of me every time I passed near the bin.

A tribute to special teachers

Mr. Tay (Primary 1 and 2) – I did not remember much about my form teacher at that time, but my mother told me that he went the extra mile to help me. For instance, he waited in class for me to finish packing my bag very slowly. I remembered that after he left, the bullies began to target me.

Mr. Tay (Primary 4, another teacher) – Once, I was angry with a classmate for not befriending me any more. He was supposed to be my best friend and but he sided with the bullies instead. I decided to hide one of his books behind the cabinet every day during recess so that the teacher will punish him. This went on for 2 days. On the 3rd day, the class prefect caught me red-handed. I was worried about what would happen to me afterwards. The teacher spoke to me alone, asking me why I did this. I was not sure how to reply. Sensing my speech problems and that I did not have malicious intent, he told me that it was not right to do this, and the police will catch me if I tried it again. He closed the case and never mentioned it again.

I did not understand the meaning of my wrongdoing. However, during the civics and moral lesson conducted in Mandarin later in the day, the class had to study a story about villains. [In Chinese, the word for villain is literally "small person".] I made the connection between what I did and what a villain would do, and then I decided that I do not wish to be a villain. Hence, I vowed never to take revenge again. This was a miracle because even until my Polytechnic days, I did not *emotionally* understand how stories about other people connected with my personal life.

At the end of the year, Mr. Tay presented every student with a special trophy with his name carved on it. This was highly unusual because no other teacher I knew has done this. I thought that since I was such a bad boy, I would not be getting any. However, he reserved the last trophy for me. When I took the trophy, I was stunned. Although I did not understand the concept of forgiveness, I felt a deep comfort and relief.

Mr. Er (Secondary School) – Mr. Er was well read and articulate on many matters. He exposed his class to current affairs and politics outside the syllabus. When I asked him why people do not just sit on the fence and avoid taking sides, he replied me that it was difficult to do so in the real world. By showing me a new world beyond the textbook, he helped me create my destiny.

Advice

How to stop bullying?
I have no complete answer to this question. I know that people bully others because they are hurt themselves, and many people are hurt today. I can only suggest going to a good school where the students come from a happier and more caring family background. However, if the autistic is high functioning enough, it might be possible for him to build an alliance with a group of empathetic friends through gifts and contributing

important help. Bullies tend to prey on lone individuals. They hesitate when they see a group of people who will protect their potential victim.

I wish to emphasize that bullying is not just a problem for autistic children. It happens to many different people at all ages. While it might be possible to control bullying in school with teachers, it is not possible to stop bullying in adult society by asking the government to intervene. Choosing a suitable social environment and developing an alliance with protective friends may be the only way to avoid bullies.

Will speech and drama help?
Many people believe that art and drama will help autistics. I tend to disagree because I believe that these are of little help until the autistic is ready (with enough of his instincts activated to appreciate and understand these). Making the autistic a character in a school performance does not mean he will become better at social skills. The actors have to rehearse thoroughly before the play. During the play, everything has to happen like clockwork according to the script. These remind me of an autistic's ideal social scenario.

Will art help?
Art necessarily bring out the creative qualities of an autistic. Some autistics have natural talents in art, which wise parents can channel into useful skills (such as advertisement design or architecture). For autistics like myself who do not appreciate or do art well, I suggest focusing on other matters until our instincts are ready.

Will social skills training help?
I am hesitant to recommend social skills training, especially on etiquette, because training by rote without instinctive understanding or desire only makes social life a chore rather than a pleasure. I believe that when his instincts are ready, the autistic will pick up many important social skills with his own effort. However, if his instincts are not ready, then he can only pretend to know and try to cope.

Will fictional stories help?
In the case of fiction, I believe that what works for non-autistic children often will not work for autistics. Fairy tales only confuse me. Why did the

nose of Pinocchio keep growing longer when he lies? How can people transform into swans with the wave of a magic wand? Ignorant of both the morale of the story and the concept of metaphors, I fail to find any scientific basis that can make sense to me. I still had difficulty telling fact from fiction even as a teenager. If the story is set in a magical kingdom or different era, I will treat it as fiction. However, I often react to stories set in the modern era on planet Earth as if they are real.

I do not recommend showing fictional material to autistics unless there is a good reason. This is especially the case for video material, which can easily induce the autistic to imitate or make his imagination go awry. If such materials are used, I suggest that parents and teachers should:
- Choose to share only wholesome stories
- Choose stories which are obviously not real (i.e. set in a different era)
- Choose TV shows and movies that have no cruelty or violence
- If stories are realistic, then explain clearly that they are make-believe

Give breathing space
People forget that autistics need time to think, and may find it difficult to answer their questions or reply to their argument. My mother was prone to pile one argument onto another when she talked to me, expecting me to answer her quickly. When I complained, she reminded me that when I go to work as an adult, my boss would not be so forgiving.

Sometimes autistics need a place to rest from all the social business and be alone. This may be as simple as hiding in a quiet corner to read a book. In Secondary School, I had a special shelter (codenamed "L3") just above the teacher's room where I would go every recess right after my meal and read my book. I also had another shelter (codenamed "L4") further away on the highest floor in my school, which I may go if I am eating bread and it is not raining. I liked to observe the other children playing from a distance without them noticing my presence.

Near the end of Secondary school, I joined a 3-day astrology discovery camp and discovered that all the social games and activities drained me too much. I asked the facilitators for a break, but as everyone else was keen to continue, they declined my request. I could only struggle on to exhaustion.

Provide written instructions
If only my teachers would write their instructions down instead of saying it. If only I can memorize the name of my classmates with photograph labels instead of calling out names verbally. If only I could react by email instead of face-to-face interviews, life would be far less stressful for me.

Find or become the best friend of the child
I do not need 100 friends. Even today, I prefer to keep to myself and have less social interaction. A best friend and two good friends was more than enough for me. It is the quality, not the quantity, which matters to me.

C5: MY BODY & ENVIRONMENT

Human limitations were too severe for me to take. I wish to break free of this frail and sickly body. Soar to the stars. Transform myself into anything I like. Make all wishes come true in an instant. Melt into the programming system of reality and start changing the laws of physics.

Human technology is too primitive. Humans are proud of their puny supercomputers, fragile fighter jets, wobbly skyscrapers and inaccurate GPS satellite system. Yet they are still at the mercy of mere hurricanes, earthquakes and diseases. Those who escape still die of old age in mere decades. Their economical system is driving their wildlife to extinction. Their political system seems bent on driving themselves to extinction.

I see before me, a crazy civilization stranded on a tiny blue planet. I see a civilization unaware of the infinite possibilities of outer space, desperately trying to protect minute pieces of their planet from each other. I see chaos and suffering where people attack, cheat or kill each other for sheets of paper (i.e. money), ideological logos, small parcels of land and mating partners.

I detested the dirt, the noise and the ugliness around me. The mucus coming from my nose and throat... Yuck! Human bodies also need rest, food and maintenance. What a hassle! If only I could photosynthesize like a plant or run on electricity so that I can save time eating and going to the toilet. Even worse, this body breaks down over time, with many irreplaceable parts. In mere decades, it would be hard to operate and uglier than ever.

Events on Earth take time: not nanoseconds, but years! I cannot teleport and clone myself at will. I must express myself in imprecise words instead of telepathic knowing. It is beyond human power to memorize every book in the National Library, when even a simple computer can do so easily.

Marooned on this isolated backwater, I felt that my real home lies far beyond the stars. I could not accept my identity as an Earthling, my home as Planet Earth, and my human body with its severe limitations. Such thoughts made it difficult for me to accept Humanity.

Main Issues

Lack Physics Instinct

Non-autistics have a special class of instincts that I collectively call the Physics Instinct. This instinct allows people to function smoothly in 3-dimensional space. It enables our mind to create the following experiences:

1. **Form**: The shape and structure of an object
2. **Texture**: How the object feels to touch
3. **Mass**: Gravity's effect on the object
4. **Location**: The place where the object exists
5. **General Behavior**: How an object may behave (e.g. glasses will break if they fall, a stick will move in a certain manner when thrown)
6. **Predictive Behavior**: What might happen to an object in an observed situation (e.g., A glass placed at the edge of a table is likely to fall and break. We instinctively feel uncomfortable and move it to safety.)
7. **Bodily Awareness**: The location, state and "space of mobility" of all our body parts

This instinct is pervasive: it colors people's consciousness no matter if they are waking, dreaming or imagining something. It makes physics processing so effortless that they need not constantly think about how to move their hands. With a malfunctioning physics instinct, I lacked depth perception. The world appeared to me like a flat TV screen. I had no idea where my body was and how I could use it to modify my environment. When I perform daily tasks like stapling paper or pouring water, I used my eyesight to guide me. Any distraction means another accident.

In addition, the behavior of objects was a mystery to me. How would I know that placing glass objects close to the edge of the table might cause accidents? How do I know that I should put knives facing away from people, because someone might cut himself taking it out or it might drop? How do I know that slamming the cupboard doors may cause it to break and come loose? I only knew if someone warns me verbally.

I knew that I had this handicap only when I started recovered from it. One day around 2003, I spontaneously began to sense something different about the world. It seems that objects are "floating" and "popping out". It took me over a week to get used to this. At the same time, my audio-visual-smell imagination also developed a bodily-touch component. I began to understand why most people could work so easily with physical objects.

Hardly Enjoy Bodily Experiences

I could only experience very low quality pleasure. It felt "distant" and detached, as if I was not one experiencing them. Its intensity was far less than 10% of what I feel today. However, I experienced negative sensory experiences at 60% to 80% of today's intensity. When I ate, any unpleasant taste or texture easily overwhelmed the little pleasure I felt. As most foods induced displeasure or are not worth the processing effort (e.g. remove skin and bones), I preferred to play safe and avoid any food that I have never tested before. I resented my mother's attempts to introduce "weird" food to my diet.

Not only was I unable to enjoy the joy of companionship, but I had no idea of the joy of doing nothing but just relaxing. I could only experience mental pleasures, such as the excitement of inventing something (e.g. my Yunilen Phonetic System), the thrill of making a new discovery or the awe of seeing the beautiful patterns in knowledge. This encouraged me to focus exclusively on the mental realm and ignore the physical realm of suffering.

I could feel pleasure from certain harmonious music. I started to realize that when I hear such music, my imagination presents a beautiful movie with complex spirals and abstract patterns. For particularly evocative songs, I would see a metaphoric music video, such as a cow wearing construction clothes jumping over the moon. I felt a mild ecstasy as this happened, but I did not become obsessed with it.

During my visit to Macau in 2006, I opened up to new sensory experiences. Tasting new food, I started to appreciate the mixture of flavors that contribute to the unique experience of food, including the supposedly unpleasant ones. As I held hands, hugged and gently kissed some of my new friends, I experienced the pleasures and warmth of companionship. This was a welcome relief to my old life in Singapore where I was mostly alone.

Sensitive Hearing
I have sensitive hearing and could hear my mother coming down the stairs to my apartment block. I can also detect high frequency sounds, like the buzzing from CRT TV sets. I knew when someone switches on the TV nearby, even with the volume muted. My Polytechnic once installed a huge TV set in front of the library that made a very loud irritating buzz. I quickened my footsteps every time I passed by it. However, students apparently deaf to this noise were waiting there for their friends! [Fortunately, LCD TV sets do not have this problem.]

In Secondary School, I realized that if I paid attention, I could determine if someone is close behind me. Some friends tried to surprise me by coming from my back, but I sensed them and turned around to surprise them instead. [Later, I read a science article about a theory that our ears actually emit sound to help us navigate our environment. This could explain how I felt their presence.]

Flicker Sensitivity
I can often see CRT computer monitors flicker. They look like an unstable mirror, shaking and distorting itself. Using such monitors for more than a few minutes often give me headaches. Fortunately, I know how to increase the frequency to remove the flicker. I can still see a small horizontal wave at 72Hz, a very subtle line at 75Hz, and no anomalies at 85Hz. [Fortunately, LCD monitors do not have this problem.]

Disease Warning Instinct
Around 2006, I could feel my body becoming unwell, warning me of impending illness. I could also feel my throat drying up and becoming irritated, warning me of throat infection. When this happens, I will rest and drink lots of water. My mother used to scold me for not informing her

of impending illnesses until it was too late. She told me to be more sensitive to my body, but without this instinct, I could not understand how to do so.

Illness
I was a sickly child. My stomach was often bloated due to indigestion. My mother often checked my stomach for excess air, then apply medicinal oil to aid digestion. I also had asthma. My mother's verbal explanation was useless in helping me expel the mucus in my throat and lungs. I resorted to coughing very violently to force these out. Fortunately, I completely recovered after Primary 4.

I had a runny nose almost every day, even in the Army. In order to save money, I made small and compact rolls of toilet paper for sneezing that I kept in my school bag and pocket. I had low blood pressure and my body felt very cold to the touch although its body temperature tested normal. I only felt my body warmth sometime during my Army Days.

Coping with Poor Bodily Control
I have a coping strategy in which I program my body like a robot. Firstly, I consider possible strategies of how to accomplish the task. Then, I choose the fastest strategy. As I execute each step, I quickly crunch the coordinates and actions necessary to accomplish it. I rely on my eyesight for feedback, so I must always pay attention or accidents will occur. In my Polytechnic, I visualized arrows and bars to help guide my movements more precisely.

Removing fish bones was a major engineering challenge. I must survey the fish for bones and begin excavation work. After the bones are exposed, I must remove them as quickly as possible. Even so, I often missed bones and found it difficult to spit them out later. After I refused to eat bony fish due to the unacceptable waste of time, my mother decided to remove the bones for me instead. My mother misunderstood my refusal as that I did not know how to eat bony fish.

Coping with Illness

Diet

My mother had her own way of treating me of asthma – she would put me on a special diet that eliminates (1) spicy food, (2) sweet food, (3) cold food, (4) sour food and (5) food with excessive artificial chemicals (e.g. potato chips and certain cookies). In addition, after dinnertime, I could not eat sticky food (e.g. cake and biscuits that tend to stick to the throat walls) or else I might develop sore throat and fever within days. Sometimes my mother cooked instant noodles for my supper (without the packets of flavoring). Unfortunately, even plain noodles are enough to cause a bad bout of sneezing the next day.

Food available to me included fish porridge, plain white bread (with the darkened skin peeled off), white rice, vegetables, chicken, fish and noodles. After eating, I must always drink a cup of warm water to clear my throat. As I could not drink cold water, I carried a thermos flask in my school bag.

To save money, my mother avoided unnecessary luxuries. Unfortunately, she sometimes buys (probably discounted) foods I disliked. They include:
- Squid: a strange and yucky-looking dish
- Fish: with lots of bones getting in the way
- Boney meat: what a hassle removing the bones
- Fatty meat: disgusting

Although many foods (especially meat) have some kind of odd taste that repelled me, my mother demanded that I eat all the food on the table. I tried to comply, but there are limits to how disgusting, awful or troublesome the food can be. It was a pity that I could not appreciate my mother's excellent cooking skills.

Swimming

My mother sent me for swimming lessons, believing that swimming strengthens my lungs.

Medicine

My mother relied extensively on antibiotics and Western medicine to treat me. She never relied on holistic therapies or Traditional Chinese Medicine. Aware of antibiotic resistant diseases, she required me to follow the prescription instructions closely. Knowing that I could not explain myself, she went with me to the doctor and explained the disease symptoms for me. She became so expert on my health that sometimes she would recommend a prescription. She accompanied me until I decided to go by myself in 2005. This surprised the family doctor.

Notable Incidents

Talked without closing mouth: In Primary school, my mother often told me to close my mouth as I speak. I did not realize that people could not understand me because I did not use my lips to help me pronounce words clearly. As I did not understood what she meant, I made no improvement. However, in Secondary school, the problem went away by itself.

Distorted sense of touch: In Secondary school, a female classmate brushed her hand against mine accidentally. She was attractive and I would have enjoyed that experience today. However, at that time I felt the strong disgust. I avoided touch, with the exception of shaking hands.

Advice

Use high quality products: For careless autistics, I believe that it is more cost effective to buy something very durable but more costly than something cheap but of low quality. I also suggest that they use military grade notebooks such as the Twinhead Durabook series.

Avoid difficult tasks: Sometimes it is less frustrating for everyone to avoid unnecessary difficult psychomotor tasks like eating very bony fish. For those that we cannot avoid, practice helps to make perfect.

Address sensory needs: Earplugs may help. We can improvise hidden, disposable earplugs out of a small lump of tissue paper. Hint: Sometimes the psychological effect is sufficient.

C6: COMMUNICATION & RELATIONSHIPS

"*Who am I?*" I did not know. I was not awake. I did not exist. The legs moved. The mouth spoke. The hands wrote pencil markings. Except for loops of nursery songs that sometimes kept playing, the mind was quiet. It lived without past or future. Just being here, and being now. It obeyed instructions it could understand. It reacted to things that it knew. It worked on automatic. Perhaps people thought that an invisible barrier has trapped the child. But who was trapped? There was no one who can answer the doorbell.

In Secondary 3, I was born when I read a book that declared, "*Take control of your life. You can create your future!*" Without conscious thought, I can only obey this command. However, I found it conflicting with another command issued by my teachers and parents. The former told me to select subjects that interested and benefited me. The latter wanted me to study the standard syllabus and focus only on grades. Finding it impossible to obey both commands, I must choose one of them. As I did so, I woke up.

The people around me pressured me to choose the other command. I resisted. The more I resisted, the more I awakened. Coming to experience individuality, I knew that I have chosen different from others in my choices, beliefs and knowledge. I knew that I had a past and a future. I discovered my creativity – the power to make things that never existed before.

After the sublime euphoria of birth, I found myself alone and vulnerable. I was too different from everyone else. I could not find anyone to share my mental space. I started to think that I was an alien marooned on Planet Earth. I literally had a different consciousness because my sense of self only included my mind. This human body is but an alien exploration vehicle, and its emotions are unwanted defects. The "real me" observed everything from a vantage point far away, like a NASA technician operating a robotic vehicle on Mars.

Feeling that humans were too primitive and downright silly, I wanted to better their lot. I decided to commit myself to creating a huge, international research lab that would solve every problem that Humanity faced. I set a goal for myself to earn $10 million Singapore dollars by age 25 and US$10 billion by age 35 to create this lab.

I also went on a one-boy campaign to change the Singapore Educational System. However, the people around me either ignored or laughed off my ideas and thoughts. I ignored them. Disillusioned with school life, I wanted to stop studying after secondary school. However, my mother insisted that I obtain a Diploma from a Polytechnic. I followed her wishes grudgingly, justifying it as paying off my debt to her for rearing me.

Meanwhile, I went on the Internet to share my new ideas with lengthy debates and articles. I started a new field of study named the Theory of Sociologistics, a new systems theory about how to build efficient societies that could accommodate all ideals and beliefs. I believed that Humanity needed a completely new understanding of social systems and organization in order to make World Peace feasible. Instead of participating in my extremely important project, many people on the Internet responded with ridicule and flame mails.

Although frustrated, I doubled my efforts with new research projects and more articles. As the only known person who noticed the social problems and wanted to make a difference, I carried a great responsibility. Even if no one else is willing to save the planet, I must still try my best. One of my ambitious projects was to invent a better language to replace the primitive Earth languages. I failed in this and invented a new phonetic system instead.

After I received my diagnosis of autism, I felt hurt that other people have treated me badly. To make up for this, I declared that autistics are superior morally, mentally and logically. My self-esteem skyrocketed. I became arrogant and disdainful of anything "practical", and of anyone who dared question my potential and skills. When I tried to rally the autistics on the Internet to join my cause, I started realizing that many of them are bickering, emotionally disturbed and divided by their own version of politics. To me, this seemed even worse than the world of the non-autistics. Unable to muster any solid support, I gave up on this quest.

In 2002, a new friend introduced me to the inspiring (but controversial) works of Neale Donald Walsch. This material revealed to me the meaning and beauty of life on planet Earth. Trusting in a Higher Power, I released my anxieties and worries. Soon after, the Singapore Army drafted me. My colleagues were friendly and helpful, forgiving my social mistakes and giving me opportunities to grow. I had many opportunities to observe office life close-up and practice being competent and reliable.

My feelings became intense and chaotic, yet also more subtle and varied. Sometimes, raging anger against injustice filled me. Sometimes, the soft motherly love for all living creatures overflowed my heart. The former swept through my consciousness like a violent hurricane, the latter, like a fragrant perfume. When made decisions, I felt the pain of free will: for every choice we make, we must sacrifice something else.

These experiences gave me an intuitive understanding of the lives of humans. Knowing what other people must have gone through, I developed respect and concern for them. Feeling their emotions as mine, I responded to them. A colleague summed it up in her parting words before I left the Army: "*When you first came, you were a jerk. Now, you are my close friend.*"

Self Consciousness

Much as a person who cannot see color is color-blind, I was "people blind". This blindness arose from my incomplete awareness of myself as a human being. I spent much of my childhood in a state much like sleepwalking. Even when I developed self-awareness, it was mental: I was still mostly unaware of my emotions and body. In this situation, how is it possible for me to understand and emphasize with other people, when I could not even do the same for myself?

I believe that to understand the concept of "other minds", we need to understand the concept of "our mind" first. The total experiencing of our thoughts, emotions, behaviors and reactions is the foundation for understanding the same processes in other people. In other words, it is not the "theory of other minds" that I needed, but the "experience of my mind". Simplified social skills training and rule-based decision-making cannot substitute for this process.

Subjective Personal History
Non-autistics create a personal story explaining who they are and how they came to be. This helps them understand their motivation and decide what to do in the future. It also gives meaning to their lives.

My Personal History started only when I developed self-awareness. Under the influence of self-help books, I saw myself a creative genius that could handle any problem that life threw at me. This evolved into a story of a brave, lone warrior who wished to save the world as well as a genius who have great contributions to make, if only other people would support him.

Human Intentions
I believe that self-conscious autistics are capable of developing original thinking, but it does not mean they can benefit from such creativity.

Someone invented handles for cups because he (or she) discovered that holding a hot cup would scald his hand. A trolley may have handles, brakes and a latch allowing it to fold up so that the human user will find it convenient to use. Hotels set good examples for students of "Human Intentions" because they do everything with the comfort and convenience of their guests in mind.

Most people confine their creativity to (1) what works for humans, (2) what cultural norms expect and (3) what has worked before. Autistics do not have this inhibition and are free to invent anything. Unfortunately, this means that most of their inventions are unsuitable for human needs or unpalatable to human tastes.

"Future Sense"
The lack of understanding of human intentions goes beyond invention. An extension of "human intentions" is the "Reactive Predictive Instinct" or the "future social sense". For instance, when you think of washing your hands in the same area that someone is washing dishes, you may

immediately realize that water may splash onto the other person and make her upset. When you think of tying shoelaces in a busy passageway, you may sense that you will obstruct the paths of many people and possibly upset them.

This seemingly psychic ability guides non-autistics in their every action and thought to prevent social conflicts. I discovered this instinct when I was about to cross a road in 2005. Seeing that a speeding car was approaching me, I took a step backwards. I sensed that the driver would notice my intention of not crossing the road, so he would not slow down to avoid knocking me down. In this way, he took less time to drive past, allowing me to cross the road faster. After this, I understood that human beings use non-verbal communications to communicate not facts, but intentions. When I monitor my social interactions, sometimes I see a short flash of potential future reactions. A handful of scenes may flash by in less than half a second before my subconscious selects one of them for use. This instinct is so useful that I wondered how I managed to live without it for so long.

Mutual Negotiation / Compromise
I once lacked the ability to negotiate or compromise with other people. Such skills require empathy and experience with "Human Intention".

On an overseas trip, I once shared the same room with an autistic friend. He wanted to pack his belongings at 2:30 a.m. while I tried desperately to sleep. Unable to bear it anymore, I confronted him and told him to continue his packing in the morning. He refused, stating that it will only take another half an hour. I told him that his packing was disturbing my sleep. He replied that he did not see how I would be disturbed. Ignoring me, he continued packing. The next day, we had to fetch water from the river after we bathed. When I started filling the pails, he left abruptly without any explanation. I thought that he was not going to help, but 20 minutes later, he finished whatever he was doing and returned with two pails of water. If I did not know about autism, I would not want to befriend this person again.

In Macau, I broke certain unspoken house rules. I was not supposed to eat directly from a pot or pan after cooking. I did so because I could save on washing dishes and reduce wastage incurred when transferring food to a plate. Seeing this, my housemates told me, "*a pot or pan is used for cooking and bowls and plates are meant for eating*". A few years ago, I would reject this as illogical and refuse to comply, but no longer. There are also rules about the equal division of work. I thought that helping housemates in technical areas and computers might exempt me from housework, but changed my mind when I saw their delight when I mopped the floor. Still, this may be reasonable because I could not help in important chores like cooking. I also knew that my housemates must have already put up with many of my quirks, and only confronted me about the most disturbing ones. The least I can do is to put up with their requests or quirks too.

Some people thought that I was selfish because I only cared for myself. Not knowing that I was socially unaware, people did not bother to list out their compromises and sacrifices for me. When I did not know about these, I can only see myself compromising and sacrificing for others. Why must I always help people, when they never seemed to contribute anything to me? That sounds rather unfair.

People sometimes complain that I never show respect. This is part of the same issue. Not seeing the deeper implications of their sacrifices, contributions, experiences and abilities, I wonder why I should respect someone simply because of an order. In fact, I thought of respect as irrational, mindless conformity to authority figures.

Belonging / Tribal
Most non-autistics took for granted the instinct that fosters their sense belonging to a family, race, culture, religion or country. Ignorant of this, I wondered why my classmates form small cliques consisting of 2 to 5 members. My classmates' habit of supporting football leagues and having idols also made no sense to me. However, when I went to the Army, I needed a coping strategy because I did not know how to join a clique. Not having a group to shelter me, I was an easy target of bullies. My mother told me to bring extra food and tools when I was in the boot camp to share with my fellow bunkmates. It paid off when they saved me from a potentially serious bullying incident.

When I went to work in the Army office, I decided to follow the Singapore model. Like people, the international community also has its cliques. Instead of joining only one of them, Singapore chose to maintain excellent relationships with everyone, including the USA and China (PRC). Despite its small size, it receives strong support from the international community.

Knowing that I was at the bottom of the pecking order because of my rank, I set forth to befriend everyone in the department. My mother encouraged me to buy little gifts such as sweets as a substitute for my poor social skills. I also did my part to reduce my autistic tendencies with a pleasant personality who apologized for mistakes, did my best in my work and help people whenever I can. I also made an effort to learn from and listen to advice from other people. However, because I have yet to develop emotional bonding, I never felt that I was part of the team. I considered team bonding and building games as irrelevant.

It was only when my grandfather died that I felt for the first time what it meant to be part of a family, and what it felt like to have someone in the family depart. When I led the other grandchildren in the funeral possession, I felt for the first time what it feels like to be the elder brother, having the responsibility to guide all the younger siblings along the correct path.

The tribal instinct helps us to know where we belong, where "our home" is and where "our people" are. When I did not have it, I never felt that I belonged anywhere. Lacking the feeling of motherly bond, I did not feel that my mother is my mother. It is not that I did not love my mother, but that I treated all people equally. What I would do for my mother, I would do for anyone else in the same situation.

Secondary Issues

Mostly Mental Relationships
Non-autistics tend to develop relationships with each other, and live for those whom they love. Take away companions, and you take away much meaning from their life. Many autistics tend to develop relationships with

the mental realm, and live for those ideas, discoveries and knowledge that they love. Take away these, and you take away much meaning from their lives.

Both parties might judge each other harshly for their choice of relationship. However, I feel that both kinds of relationships are part of the human experience. Those who experience both will experience a richer part of the human experience.

Setting Priorities

I did not understand the intention behind the tasks I do. I did not know how they relate to each other in time and strategic importance. As a result, every task was equally important, and every mistake equally serious. The problem of how to handle tasks constantly bothered me. Not knowing that instincts and simplicity held the key to mastery, I tried to build a program based on the Windows 2000 kernel task scheduling system. It never worked for me.

My old working style failed in the Army when I worked for multiple superiors. Treating everything as equally important, I could not deliver work as quickly as my superiors wanted. In my effort to adapt, I observed other people and modified my internal scheduling system. With a simple system based on meeting the nearest deadlines and avoidance of unnecessary work, I managed to keep my superiors happy most of the time.

Today, I maintain 2 planning systems. The first is a typical appointment system for me to record events and reminders. The second is a computer-based notepad with a list of tasks to do. When I finish my tasks, I erase it from the notepad. This system worked pretty well for me.

Elaborating on the Reactive Predictive Model

The "future social sense" is the foundation for a communication model called "Reactive Predictive Communications" (RPC). Non-autistics use this model subconsciously to guide them. This model has the following steps:

1. The sender constructs a simulated model of the receiver based on his understanding
2. He sends a test message to the simulated receiver
3. Analyzing the response, he tunes the message to fit the response
4. He repeats steps 2 to 3 until he has the appropriate response
5. He then transmits the specially constructed message to the 'real' sender

Here is an example of the process:
1. Alice wants to tell Jack to stop bothering her by blowing his nose loudly
2. Alice constructs a test message: "Stop blowing your nose loudly"
3. Alice *imagines* saying this message to Jack and observing his reaction
4. *Imaginary* Jack refuses to listen
5. Alice tries a different message taking into account Jack's preference: "I will give you a chocolate if you stop sneezing loudly"
6. *Imaginary* Jack accepts the offer but breaks his promise
7. Alice repeats the above steps until she gets the expected response from *imaginary* Jack: compliance
8. Alice communicates final message to the *real* Jack: "I will not let you copy my homework if you keep sneezing so loudly"

In RPC, the reaction is the message. RPC works on the principle that everyone is constantly influencing the people around them through their words and actions. In other words, human beings do not operate as separate individuals, but a collective entity that I call the "group body". This encourages people to set aside their personal differences and work together to achieve common goals.

While people often rely on emotions to decide, they use logic to justify them. While they have differences in choices and preferences, they avoid overt display of differences or desires, such as verbally stating an order. To protect group harmony, they can choose to give non-verbal clues, put a spin on certain information or omit certain details to induce others to oblige. This is not really lying: this is part of the human instinct of making peace.

Experiments on split-brain patients and involuntary simulation of neural implants suggest that we do this to ourselves all the time! When experimental subjects moved because the researcher simulated their brain, they could always explain away their actions. When split-brain patients were shown two conflict images to both sides of the brains so that both their hands pointed at two conflicting objects, they had an explanation.

In contrast, autistics use a different communication model called "Straight Forwards Communication" (SFC). In SFC, the data is the message. Like computers, autistics aim to inform each other of information, opinions and thoughts. With logic as their core matter, the autistic appears to talk above or past the non-autistic on matters with no relevance or influence. Unfortunately, SFC is not a viable approach. Human beings use audio speech, a very slow medium compared to fiber-optic cables. Human communications cannot function without compressing most of their data exchange into assumptions and non-verbal signals.

Coping Strategies

"Redirected" Eye Contact: Although my mother has trained me to look at people during conversations, she could not teach me how to make eye contact. I only knew how to stare at people, which was highly uncomfortable and disorientating. Instead, I searched for a high contrast feature around, beside or behind their eyes that I could lock my gaze on, such as a bright earring, a dark mole or a red thumbtack on a white notice board. Later on, my instincts made it possible for me to use "soft focus" eye contact. However, it took me at least a year to feel comfortable using it.

Reduce social contact to minimum: Even today, I often found myself facing too many social demands. I needed all my time for my career and work. Hence, I avoid social contact, especially when I am busy or stressed out.

Use email: I used to like communicating exclusively by email, because the written form clarifies logic and gives me time to reflect and think. I can also avoid unproductive emotional-laden exchanges with people. However,

I found online text chatting too intrusive. Nowadays, I prefer face-to-face meetings because I feel goodwill and reassurance when I meet people.

Advice

Observe and Imitate: Showing the autistic child how to observe and imitate other people so that they will know what to do is a good idea.

Appoint a "Defense Attorney": Perhaps someone can help the child to advocate to other people what he may be feeling, thinking or intending. A less direct way is to help monitor if teachers or parents are losing patience. If so, the advocate can remind them to calm down, explain to the child and give him time to reflect.

Notable Stuff

Online Nickname: Man-Go
When we hear sounds, they create an emotional reaction in us. Hence, advertisers take great care in choosing the names for their products in order to strike the "right note". When I first went on the Internet in secondary school, I chose the nickname "Man-Go". I thought that it was a masculine nickname because the word "man" was in it. Unfortunately, most people thought that I was female.

Potential Romance in Polytechnic
I remember a female classmate who only met me during Physical Education lessons. She would exclaim or make certain remarks whenever the sport teacher mentioned me. For example, once I reported my height for a health report, and she exclaimed, "*Wow! So tall!*" She also stared at me in a strange way. I did not realize that it was an expression of romantic interest. In the end, she gave up and found herself a boyfriend.

I remember a teenager girl who worked in a computer shop that I patronized. One day, I asked her when a certain computer part would arrive. She gave me an intense and warm smile while her eyes locked straight onto mine. She replied in an unusual tone that the stock was not available, but I could leave my telephone number with her if I wanted. I did not do so. The computer shop has since closed down over a year ago.

Funny Jokes
In Secondary 2, I had composed the following Christmas jingle that I liked to sing often:

> Jingle Bells,
> Batman smells,
> Robin flew away,
> Superwoman lost her belt,
> Scoopy-Doopy-Doo!

While working in the Army, I found a department named "MCMD", which I renamed "Mad Cow Mad Disease". It reminded me of a government agency named "MCDS", which I nicknamed the "Mad Cow Disease Specialist". Unaware that I might cause offense, I went around telling people about my new joke.

Technical Speech
I feel comfortable using formal speech with using engineering, computer, military and sci-fi terms. I believe both my reading material and my different consciousness are responsible.

Infrequent bus schedules have unacceptable latency. I download food from the pot into a bowl, and upload them to my mouth. I ask for the ETA (Estimated Time of Arrival) and margins of error in estimation. I request an immediate evacuation of the apartment in order to arrive on time for a meeting. I activate the lights instead of switching them on. During a blackout, I will reroute emergency power (i.e. my laptop batteries) to my computer. I need to perform an FTL (Faster Than Light) jump to migrate to Australia. I need intel (intelligence) before I decide to proceed with a plan or not.

C7: EARTH TIME & PLANNING

Originally, I lived in "now-here" without past or future. My reality consisted of only what was happening in front of me. Such was my "Mirror Mind".

Although the school textbooks taught me about objective time, the abstract clock hands and numbers revealed nothing about the subjective experience of time. The past had no meaning, the present was confusing and the future was unknown. Lost in the pitch-dark hallway of time, I feared the unknown dangers that lurked ahead. Fortunately, timetables provided small beacons of light that reassured and instructed me on my journey.

After I awakened to myself, my perception of time changed. Previously, I only used time as a tool to comply with instructions or to figure out what to do. Time flowed only when I did something. If I stopped, time stopped too. After I awakened, time became a river that constantly flowed from the unseen past into the unknown future. I watched my life in the river passively from a vantage point far away, unaware of my emotional reactions to my experiences or the meaning that these held for me.

I began to experience time as a limitation, with minutes and seconds constantly slipping away from me. Try as I might, this frail body and puny mind could never catch up: There were just too many things to tick off the checklist, too many books to finish reading. As I rushed against my human limitations, I felt minutes passing as if they were hours, and hours passing as if they were a week. Living many times faster than others, I felt a desperate urge to rest. Yet I dared not slow down because I still had so much to finish.

During my teenage days, I fantasized about creating a special room. While I was in that room, time would stop outside. I would carry all my books, tools and plans with me into the room and work on them. I would have as much time as I needed to catch up with the world. I also fantasized that I could clone myself, and have lots of me doing everything I needed to do. At the end of the day, all my clones would merge so that we knew what happened to each of us. The next morning, we would split up to complete our chores again. Unfortunately, neither fantasy is possible in the real world.

I detested my past where I made too many mistakes, and my present with its terrible imperfections. I only held on to the far future, seeing it as a perfect place where I have somehow solved all my problems. This idealized future became my reality while I neglected the past, present and immediate future.

Temporal Instinct

Non-autistics can access a special category of instincts that I collectively call the Temporal Instinct. These instincts specifically affect the subjective experience, not the abstract processing of time. This means that while the autistic may excel with mathematical time, he may fail to organize his personal schedule. The temporal instinct includes the following concepts:

Causality

Non-autistics have a sense of causality: They can feel what is likely to happen based on how things develop right now. They can also see how the consequences of their actions have created an impact. Thus, they have a roughly accurate estimate of what it takes to do something, and are able to improvise and plan their lives as a result. Their accuracy improves as they accumulate more and more experiences.

I also thought that I could do all these because I did not realize that I could not accurately estimate the effort and time I needed, and the implications that followed. Not knowing the commitment and social skills needed, I thought I could date women easily because I read 3 books about this topic. I merely chose not to do so because I was too busy. Not fully understanding the foundations of cash flow and consumer demand, I thought I could do business and get rich fast because I read so many books on this topic. I merely needed an investor smart enough to spot my talent and willingness.

Partly due to the influence of self-help books, I developed an unshakable "false confidence", believing that I could do anything if only I committed myself to it. I failed because I lacked the right opportunities, or insufficient preparation. That gave me hope to silence any critics and persist with my plans, earning me a reputation for being arrogant.

Temporal Consistency (Flow of Time)
My timeline was broken, fragmented and discontinuous. My experience of time could run awry, such as with intensive time compression where I felt a few months passing in a week. I must also use every part of my time or else I would feel agitated not knowing what to do. Non-autistics experience a more consistent and stable flow of time, regulating it between anxiety (due to "lack of time") and boredom (due to "too much time").

Temporal Coordination (Multi-Tasking)
Non-autistics can handle interruption. It is easy to stop, take a rest and continue the work. Even when they have urgent business, they know that life must still go on. The dishes need washing, the floor needs mopping and the tax forms need filling.

In contrast, I worked like a steamroller. It was slow for me start on something. Unless I happen to be in the mood, I have to reconfigure my mind first before I can work on it. Once I start, it was equally hard to stop. It did not matter if my stomach was hungry or my body tired. Like a mechanical soldier, I had only one task that I must finish. When interruptions occurred, I felt an intense irritation similar to being woken in the middle of the night without good reason. All the shape-feelings and thoughts I held in my mind vanished and I had to re-compute and reconnect everything all over again.

My mother would have none of my expressions of frustration. "*Don't you make those 'zart-zart' sounds (of irritation) or complain that you are very busy. Even corporate CEOs are not as busy as you are. With such a bad attitude, you will definitely be fired in no time.*" Finding it futile to argue, I usually kept quiet. To avoid interruptions and environmental noise, I often worked late into the night.

This problem persisted until when I started writing this book. For the first time, I can accept interruptions to my writing work and get much needed rest. I noticed that my mind has created a "tree structure" with lots of lines opening up into a fountain shape. This caches a snapshot all the tasks I have left unfinished and links them to my sense of time. When I restart my tasks, this snapshot helps me resume my work and remember their state in with a small fraction of the time and effort I needed in the past.

Probable Futures

Without a filter that tells me what is more or less likely, all futures are equally probable. In fact, certain scenarios (such as a crack in the space-time continuum destroying the universe) seemed more likely because I was more interested in them. I knew that stories that had to do with magical powers, alternate worlds or different eras were not real. However, stories set in the modern era, especially those built on a valid scientific premise, often cause me to react to them as if they are real.

During Secondary school, I saw a TV show about the criminals using TV brainwashing technology to take over the world. I began to panic, wondering if I will be brainwashed too. Suddenly another part of me took control and uttered repeatedly, "*Don't worry, this is not real*". That calmed me down and I could finish the show without fuss.

I lived in fear of spy agencies, time travelers, mad scientists, terrorists, natural disasters and nasty space aliens. While most people easily dismiss these scenarios, but these were no laughing matter for me. I had to prepare myself by reading books about what to do in a disaster or emergency. Anxious thoughts would constantly run through my mind, keeping me awake at night. It often took me 3 frustrating hours to fall asleep.

In Primary school, I watched a horror movie about ghosts and could not sleep that night. I was worried about the ghost targeting me while the haunting music kept playing in my head. Another different horror movie caused me to fear dolls, because they might come alive at night when I sleep. I no longer fear dolls and the dark. When I watched anything frightening, I imagined how the director filmed the scene so that I knew it was not real. For good measure, I also imagined myself effortlessly defeating the evil entities.

Coping with Forgetfulness

I had much difficulty remembering to bring or do things. Over time, I developed some generic strategies to help me.

1. **Do it now**: I decided that I should rush to finish something immediately whenever possible. This guaranteed that I will not forget to do it and prevents the problem from deteriorating further. Unfortunately, this became an obsession: I felt a huge inner itch to finish everything left unfinished. However, this habit no longer serves me now. I have since learnt to postpone less important things and release my anxiety.

2. **Write it down**: Writing down the tasks to do on a piece of paper, and then leaving it prominently on my table ensures that I will remember to do it. In school, I use a dairy to record appointments and tasks. Today, I use an electronic version in my computer.

3. **Do everything in the same sequence**: If I needed to do something repeatedly, I can define a sequence that I follow. This becomes a habit, ensuring that I finish everything properly.

4. **Pack things earlier**: I pack what I needed to bring the night before I leave. When I wake up, I can just grab them and go.

5. **Research & print out items beforehand**: I find the map of the place I am going, check the transportation routes and print out the instructions of things that I needed to do.

6. **Put things to bring in the same place**: I put all the things I needed to bring in a cupboard or a corner. Whenever I go out, I collect everything from that place.

7. **Triple check**: Check everything, and check again. When handing in a piece of work, check and check to make sure that everything is in order. When leaving a venue, check and check again to ensure that nothing remains behind. I had a habit in my Polytechnic to help with

that: After leaving my home, I would slap my hand on my left and right pockets to ensure physically that I brought my belongings.

Coping with "False Confidence"

"False Confidence" can be a dangerous enemy to working effectively. Looking back, I suggest the following advice to avoid it:

Cap ambition with a practical start: It is OK to be ambitious, but start with plans that are simple, coherent and self-correcting. Simple plans require the least effort to implement, coherent plans require the least effort to understand and self-correcting plans require the least effort to maintain. In addition, plans offering unknown returns or those offering amazing returns for little effort are unlikely to work and may have bad intentions.

A non-autistic friend joined an affiliate network that charged membership fees far exceeding his profit. Yet he did not quit. He wanted an unknown chance to increase his income by an uncertain amount. I thought that it made more sense to buy lottery because at least there is a known chance of winning a certain amount. Personally, I do not trust affiliate networks.

Simplicity Example
For a business project, I asked for a commission of the profits instead of a simple hourly rate. My reasoning was that I wanted a fair deal for both parties, but calculating the profit can a major administrative cost as well as inconvenience.

Coherency Example
I have a small sum of money in 3 different currencies that I wish to loan a friend. I make 3 separate loans and work out a formula to charge fees based on the currency exchange rates. This proved unnecessarily complex. Instead, what I could do was to convert all the currencies into one, and charge interest to cover the currency conversion cost and risk of currency fluctuations.

Self-Correcting Example

I just moved into a new home. The real estate agent promised to fix a leaky tap. I decided to pay him in advance as a gesture of goodwill. As a result, he did not return to fix the tap despite numerous calls. However, if I had held back half the payment until he fixed the tap, it would ensure that he returned to do so.

Never use theory as a substitute for experience: Reading books is very different from actually trying out the real thing. After general reading, it is wise to learn about how people accomplish your goals in the past as well as observe how they do so today.

Know your weaknesses by experience: Results from recent experience are a far more accurate gauge of your own abilities than personal beliefs.

Never expose your weaknesses: Do not purposely challenge your weaknesses. Instead, work around or avoid them. If I cannot cope with constant and chaotic stimuli, I would not work as a cashier in a busy superstore. If I cannot do business because I trust people too easily, I can find a trustworthy and street-smart partner to deal with the people part of my work for me.

Handling Uncertainty & Change

In 2002, I read the "7 Habits of Highly Effective People" by Stephen Covey. It advised me to focus on my "Circle of Influence" – instead of wasting my time worrying or complaining, I focus on solving my problem a step at a time.

The Serenity Prayer also inspired me with its simplicity and grace: "*God, grant me the serenity to accept the things I cannot change, the courage to change the things I can, and wisdom to know the difference.*" The Heart Sutra comments on the false phenomena of the world, encouraging me to release my attachments to results: "*Form is no other than emptiness, emptiness no other than form.*"

Reflecting on these sources reduced much of my anxiety. I admit that I did not always succeed in following these advices, but I do my best.

C8: EXPLAINING TO AUTISTICS

In many ways, I was a tourist visiting Planet Earth. However, having already taken Earth Culture for granted, few people bother to explain the ways of Earthlings to me. Those who did often said things like:

1. You are wrong.
2. Stop asking and just do it.
3. Too bad. This is the way things are done here.
4. You must show respect for ‹*authority figure*›.
5. Listen to ‹*authority figure*›. He or she knows what is best for you.
6. Even ‹*famous person*› could not do it, how could you?
7. Why pursue ‹*special interest*› when your grades are so poor?
8. You are trying to run before you can even crawl.
9. Be very, very careful. *(You mean my plans are flawed? Why?)*
10. You are being taken advantage of by doing ‹*special interest*› for free.
11. Don't be so selfish. You need to think of other people first.
12. You need to be less perfect.

Some people think that I was arrogant and stubborn because I refused to listen to sensible advice. However, if they used a more logical, precise, systematic and "autistic" way of explaining, I might have listened. I only wished that people told me statements like:

1. The purpose of a conversation is not so much about exchanging facts and ideas, but influencing other people to make your life more enjoyable.

    (Reveal the hidden human concepts; Explain systematically)

2. This office runs on a hierarchy system. Your boss tells you what to do, and you do what he says. In return, he pays you a salary. This is what we all do here. If you want to join us, you will have to do follow the system.

    (Explain the concept as a trade-off or transaction)

3. You are spending 45 minutes to plan how to save 25 cents for the bus ride. Is it worthwhile?

    (Make the logical discrepancy clear)

4. I appreciate your effort in spending ‹long time› to improve ‹unimportant task›. Would you like to solve ‹more useful problem› instead?

    (Shift the focus to a more useful area)

5. I want you to do me a favor. I will do ‹list of items› for you. This required me to ‹list of sacrifices›. In return, I expect you to do ‹undesirable task›.

    (If you want the autistic to do something he dislikes without the effort of convincing him logically, then ask him to do a favor for you. List your sacrifices and how he benefits from them.)

6. Yes, it is important to spend a lot of time and effort to ‹achieve certain perfectionist standards›. Since you are so dedicated, I have a challenge for you. Can you maintain 80% of the quality with only 20% of the time spent? I will provide ‹important recognition› if you can do it.

    (Never tell an autistic to be less than perfect. Give him more challenging and useful goals. Award him with recognition.)

7. I know that you wanted to start ‹special interest project›. What fundamental understanding do you need? Tell me about ‹fundamental concept›. Can you prove to me that you can do ‹special interest project requiring fundamental concept›? Do you want to accept the challenge and design ‹a risk free trial run› to see how you do in real life?

    (Autistics often have flawed understanding and faulty planning. It is important to help them realize these flaws themselves in a non-judgmental way, than to force one's opinions on them.)

8. Most people choose to follow traditional ways because (1) they can save thinking time, (2) new methods may have hidden flaws that may be disastrous and (3) new methods need time and effort to test. For instance, last year we tried to implement ‹another new method› and found that it has ‹fatal flaw› only after ‹disastrous incident›.

    (Illustrate your explanation with real-life examples that apply in a similar situation to the autistic's workplace)

9. Your design is too difficult for us to use. You must simplify it so that it takes less than X steps and need less than X minutes to set up. In

addition, it must cater to the ‹*special needs and senior*› staff who could not meet ‹*certain demanding requirements*›.

(Remind creative autistics of the human needs of their end users)

10. If you did not check this data carefully and miss out the errors, then you would waste ‹*list of people's effort*› and may create ‹*negative personal social consequences*›. Last year, ‹*culprit*› missed out ‹*serious mistake*› and caused ‹*bad consequences*›.

    (Remind autistics of the negative impact to other people if he makes certain mistakes)

11. I am glad that you want to become a billionaire like Bill Gates. Can you tell me how Bill Gates succeeded in becoming a billionaire? What are the factors he needed to succeed? What if he lacked the 1st factor? What if he lacked the 2nd factor? ... Which of these factors do you have now? How do you test if you have these factors? How do you achieve the factors you lack while being able to fulfill ‹*list of important incidental requirements*›? Can you accept my challenge and design ‹*a risk free trial run*› to see how you do in real life?

    (I know many people who would ridicule me for my overly ambitious goals. However, would it be more productive to help me achieve these goals by guiding me to see my blind spots?)

Conclusion

I believe that good explanations go a long way in helping autistics. Those who speak without judgment show respect for the autistic. Those who let the autistic discover his own flaws helps him grow. Those who guide him to choose rather than choose for him preserve his dignity. I felt terrible and oppressed when many people around me (including certain autism professionals) treated me as less than a mature individual.

Unfortunately, I lacked the experience to understand their advice and the clarity to see their mistake. Considering them negative skeptics who refused to consider new possibilities, I ignored them. When they refused to stop, I told them off for their caustic negativity. This created dislike and ill will. I hope that by sharing these, I can help those who will follow my path to avert many unnecessary misunderstandings.

C9: FAMILY

When I was born, my mother thought hard about how to name me. She believed that names deeply influence a person's destiny. My surname is "Chen" (陈), which means "to exhibit" or "to become like". For my middle name, she chose "Yi" (毅), meaning willpower and perseverance. My last name was "Xiong" (雄), meaning heroic. Having given me such a name, does she really expect me to be an ordinary person?

My mother prided herself on having foresight. One day, while I was in Primary school, she spoke to me. "*Those classmates who bully you are the scum of society. But unlike them, you are a good boy who studies well. You are going to be a fine person.*" She then revealed her plan for me:

- Study hard
- Get good qualifications
- Find a government job (i.e. the proverbial iron rice bowl)
- Work until I retire
- Collect my pension and do whatever I want after I retire

She told me to work as a lab technician or chemist whose main role is to write reports and test vegetable and animal samples. "*Because your job only deals with inanimate objects*", she remarked, "*You will not need good social skills to pass by. You will only need to follow procedure well.*"

Not knowing anything, I agreed. I obeyed her because I could not think for myself. However, I grew up by defying her. It all started in secondary school, when I became self-aware. My teachers disregarded my campaign to change the educational system and did not justify logically why I should study their subject. I took my education into my own hands and smuggled my books into class. I refused to study for my tests and exams.

After I finished serving in the Army, I defied her to start writing a book. She often reminded me, "*Like artists, writers have no future.*" When I persisted in using my savings to print the book, she warned me, "*Your book would never sell. You think too highly of yourself.*" My book did sell, but not well enough to provide me with usable income.

After that, I tried to start an ill-fated autism and advertising business by moving out with 2 friends. Earlier on, I spent months helping them with their volunteer amateur project. In return, they promised to commit to making the business a success. They did not deliver. I moved back home, disgraced and much poorer. "*Told you so*", my mother retorted.

After that, a wealthy woman from Macau offered to sponsor my autism work in Macau and Hong Kong. She also offered to sponsor me unconditionally to study Waldorf Education in Australia, an opportunity that I have waited many years for. Unfortunately, that also did not work out. I left my sponsor and returned to Singapore. By then, my mother had little patience left.

I told her that an organization in Hong Kong was keen to buy the rights to my book, and so did an organization in Singapore. That pacified her, until both potential deals failed. Whoops... These actions certainly did not help to create a good relationship between both of us.

I was not close to my mother, because it seems that an invisible wall separated us. I could not discuss religion, politics or philosophy without starting an argument. My Mandarin was too weak to convey my more abstract ideas accurately and to handle her verbal challenges. However, she could not understand my English and the Western concepts I used. I knew that telling her my full story would be an uphill struggle, so I thought that it would be much easier to show her this book, after someone helps me translate it into Chinese.

In 2006, I told her that I would like to help the world with my autism work. She replied, "*You should have heard those housewives in the market. I doubt that people will accept your work until 50 years later at least!*" Apparently, when she was helping to raise funds for autism, some people said unkind words (without knowing that she had an autistic child).

> "*Eww! Autistics!*" (Said with disgusting look on face)
> "*Poor parents. Must be their bad karma. I wonder what sin have they committed in their past life.*"

Such unkind words must have slapped her hard. Why do something that no one appreciates? When I was on the verge of giving up on my autism work because I could not find support in Singapore, I was tempted to agree. "*Why should I work so hard to share my discoveries, when no one is willing to listen to me?*"

Things took an unexpected turn when I was invited to Macau and Hong Kong to do my autism work. My mother strongly opposed my decision, but she did not have the heart to stop me. She helped me carry my books to the post office for mailing to Macau, gave me some spending money and sent me to the airport. In Macau, some of the most difficult times are those when I called home. My mother would often nag me about the futility of doing charity work and writing books.

"*You are wasting your youth doing useless work. You should get a decent job right now, or else after you are 28 years old, no one will want to hire you.*" I replied that it was more important to seize the day (i.e. *carpe diem*). She retorted, "*Who is going to take care of you after I die?*" I remarked that I am capable of taking care of myself. "*If I need money, I will get money. There will be a way.*"

"*What big words you have*", she taunted. "*What about all those weird projects and businesses that you were so confident of? They all failed; every single one of them!*" I replied, "*That was then, now is now. I have become wiser and more experienced.*"

"*Is it?*" my mother remarked. "*You will find that you have missed something out in your calculations. You don't know enough about how things work, and you will only bang your head if you insist.*" Such arguments were endless and drained me of what little energy I had trying to cope with my other issues in Macau.

Now that I have decided to follow my mother's advice to find a job and found some kind help to translate my book, it may not be long before I reconcile with her. I see my mother as the final frontier in my relationship development. She is so near, yet so far away. She is my closest, yet most distant person. If I can break the Invisible Wall, it would be perhaps the greatest achievement I have ever made.

Parental Control

Many autistics surrender their decision making power to their parents at an early age. This encourages parents to assume control over their lives. The autistic may then develop a lifelong habit of reliance on their parents for decision-making. It is wise for the parents to encourage the child to become independent to the extent that they are ready.

If their child goes to mainstream school, the parents may develop their own "surveillance network" consisting of other parents and classmates. This homemade version of Big Brother helps to ensure the safety of their child, but can become very invasive and may stunt the will of the child if maintained for too long. Fortunately, my mother loosened control of her network in Primary 4, setting the stage for me to rebel in Secondary 3.

Sister

I have never played the role of an elder brother in the family. My younger sister lived with me throughout my life in Singapore. She has adapted to me: She spoke English in a more formal way with me than with her friends. She also knew most of the special terminology I use. Sometimes, she criticized me for making obvious social mistakes such hurting my mother's feelings.

However, I find it most interesting that I did not treat my sister as a sibling, but rather more like a colleague with whom I had a friendly professional relationship. When I confessed to her my past feelings, she replied, "*Brother, don't be silly. How can your sister be your colleague?*" I felt relived that the feeling was not mutual.

In Macau, two Filipino mothers in Macau adopted me as their younger brother. I had the privilege of calling them "Ate", meaning "elder sister". Helping and sharing with each other gave me a very special, sublime experience of belonging. One of the special moments was during dinnertime, when we all sat together. Although I did not understand most of the conversations (in Filipino), I am aware of the special bond. At that time, I have never experienced this with my real family in Singapore.

C10: MONEY

I came from a poor family. At my old home in Primary school, we were the only apartment in the whole block that still did not have an air conditioner. Not having enough money for household expenses, my parents often quarreled late into the night. My hardworking mother also took odd jobs to supplement her income. My mother taught me, through her own example and verbally, the importance of money. The values include:

1. Avoid spending money unnecessarily
2. Save money in the bank for a rainy day
3. Do not waste food and other resources

She gave me enough money for my allowance, even if she may not have enough herself. Unlike many parents, she allowed me to keep the money I received in my red packets during Chinese New Year. She then helped me open a savings account at the Bank of China and encouraged me to save money. Later on, I closed that account and opened one closer to my Primary school. One of the bankers was particularly fond of me and always served me when I made a deposit every week.

In contrast, I knew many friends who came from well off families. They took a carefree attitude towards money. In Primary school, they tend to spend their money on good food, game cards, magazines, toy racing cars, etc. From secondary school onwards, it was girlfriends, fashion accessories, expensive dinners, concert tickets and taxi trips. In my Polytechnic, some classmates could spend SGD$1000 (US$650) on a phone and make over SGD$300 of calls every month. Although my friends may have well-paying part-time jobs, they often overspend and complain about lack of money.

I knew a classmate in Secondary school who had an allowance of SGD$10 a day, which can last me for an entire week. Unfortunately, when his family fell on hard times, he could not restrain his spending habits and had no savings to fall back upon. He had to borrow money from the bank to pay for his studies and will have to pay much interest. Such an attitude to spending money was abhorrent to me. Unlike my friends, I avoid eating out. I avoid taxis, preferring public transport unless it is an emergency. If I owe people a favor, I would rather pay with my knowledge, services and help instead of treating them for lunch.

This habit of saving became an obsession. For instance, I was very thrifty with paper. Starting from a corner, I shrank, twisted and condensed my writing so that I can use the paper for a long time before throwing it away. When I dispose of paper, I would fold it up neatly so that it does not waste space while other people simply crumble it into a ball. This habit is still with me today, albeit less extreme.

Using Money Wisely

When my mother saw the extreme way that I saved money, she chided me. "*This is not saving money. This is being miserly. You will never be likeable to other people if you are miserly. There are times when you cannot save on money and times when you can save*".

She then explained to me the certain situations that I cannot save money:
1. **Important Social Occasions** (e.g. entertaining friends, buying birthday gifts, giving wedding blessings, donating to funeral expenses)
2. **Things that damage my body** (e.g. buying cheap food with poor nutrition)
3. **Fair Treatment to other people** (e.g. offering a token sum of money as a gesture of appreciation when people help me)

She continued, "*When you are outside by yourself in society, you will have to entertain your friends. This is compulsory because it is the social custom. Without money, it is hard to do so. Depending on your job, you may have to spend 1/5 or more of your salary for social use. Anything less and people will not like to befriend you.*"

Not understanding the first point, I replied, "*I prefer not to spend so much money on things which are not meaningful to me (e.g. social entertainment). I can give back services in lieu of social entertainment. If I live simply, I don't need so much money.*" She retorted, "*You are wrong! You have no idea how society works!*" I refused to continue listening.

Indeed, I did not understand why those expensive restaurants always had business. I thought that sensible people could just cook for themselves or eat at cheap places. I was also puzzled why organizers gave tickets to concerts and events in pairs or fours. However, after I came to Macau, I understood. I felt what it is like to be with people, and saw just how people treated each other for lunch and dinner.

Business Adventures

After Secondary school, I tried one business idea after another. There was a time I ran a booth at a trade fair in a university. I negotiated what I believed was a good deal. Unfortunately, I was not as good a salesperson as I fancied, and I made my first business loss. The only consolation was that the stall opposite me lost more than twice as much because they did not bargain for better terms and had equally bad business.

I also tried my hand at trading computer parts. Unfortunately, I was not aware that that certain terms did not apply to my business. I must have raised eyebrows when I told people I did commodities trading. I did made a small profit buying some computer monitors at a used parts shop for SGD$25 each, moving them for 400 meters and then selling them to a computer shop for twice their price. [I did not realize that my profit would evaporate if half the monitors did not pass a test that the shop ran. Luckily, all the monitors passed.]

I bought 40 new tamagotchis at low cost after the craze died down and made a small profit. However, the 20 old obsolete hard disks that I also bought had no resale value at all.

With my newly acquired computer skills, I also sought out freelance jobs repairing computers. In the end, only this business proved consistently profitable. Over 6 years, I gradually raised my rates from a paltry SGD$25 to over SGD$100 per visit. Although I had a money-back guarantee, I only had to do that twice. One of them was because a client misinterpreted me to mean that I will fix every problem for every computer she had, while I was of the impression that I would only fix one computer per visit. Unfortunately, there was not enough business for me to consider it a real job.

I almost started a real business around 1999. Back then, broadband Internet was very expensive and worked on proprietary ADSL modems that did not allow Internet sharing with multiple computers. [At that time, we still did not have home routers yet.] LAN shops were a new concept and I only knew of two in Singapore – both used one ADSL modem per computer. While fixing a computer for a client, I had figured out a way to use a USB adapter and software router to bridge the proprietary modem interface and thus share the connection with many computers.

I mentioned this discovery to a new computer client, who recently retired and was keen to invest in something. Over the next few weeks, I wrote a business proposal and made business spreadsheets calculating operating costs and profitability. I pitched to him and his other retired friend that with our technical advantage, we could achieve significantly lower operating costs and earn back our capital as quickly as 9 months. Although my newly acquired computer skills and business studies knowledge served me well, my lack of social skills demolished the desire of a hastily created team to work with me. Due to the lack of an interested team to implement this idea, it was back to freelance computer repair for me.

Financial Independence

My mother seemed to believe that finding a stable job with good benefits and generous pension is the first key to wealth. The other is to avoid luxuries and save money. Around 1998 or so, I ran some calculations and discovered this:

Assuming that I find a job that pays a handsome salary of SGD$4000 (US$2600) a month. After subtracting taxes, government compulsory savings contributions, supporting my parents, and all expenses, I might be able to save SGD$2300 (US$1500) a month. At this rate, it will take me over 36 years to save my first million dollars.

However, my personal plan required me to obtain my first ten million by age 25, so I had only 10 years left. Thus, I considered my mother's ideas unrealistic. Rather than work part-time jobs like my friends, I tried small businesses like freelance computer services. Unfortunately, my business understanding was flawed: I had neither a practical alternative plan nor good income. On hindsight, I should have followed conventional advice to find employment to gain experience of how the world works.

During that time, I also made another calculation about financial independence: Assuming that the interest rate is 3% per year. How do I need to put in the bank to generate an interest of SGD$2500 per month as my passive income? That works out to be exactly SGD$1 million. With compound interest and an average job, I will probably need 3 decades to redeem my freedom.

Around 2004, after I read Robert T. Kiyosaki's book "Rich Dad, Poor Dad", I understood much more. The book contains useful pointers, a small part of which I will paraphrase below with my own understanding.

- Wealth is measured by how long your money lasts when you lose your job. If you have $10000 and spend $1000 a month, then your wealth is 10 months.
- Wealthy people know the trick of infinite wealth. This means that their wealth will (theoretically) last forever even if they do not work.
- Assets grow your money while liabilities eat your money.
- The trick is to have assets that can generate enough income to more than cover for all liabilities and expenses.
- Common Assets include: property (for rental), banking (to loan people money), investments (such as shares where you get dividends), intellectual property (such as patents and rights to publish books, music and movies)
- Income obtained this way is "passive", meaning money that works for you, not the other way around.
- Most people are trapped in the "rat race" of working for money. Even doctors and lawyers who earn very high incomes must keep working to get money.
- Only passive income allows us to escape this rat race and retire forever.

I told my mother some of my discoveries and argued, "*Surely, there is a future for some writers. Surely, there are ways to make a living more easily. I wish to earn money too, but it is not through a government job that I seek my fortune.*" She replied, "*You are talking big words again! Go and get a job first.*"

However, after I promised to work, I asked her about financial independence. I was surprised when she said, "*Yes, if you save enough money, you can buy property and earn money from the rising property prices*". I replied that I preferred to rent it out for passive income and she agreed that it was feasible.

After I crunched some statistics from the Internet, I found that property rental offered a much better rate of return than the bank. As little as SGD$450,000 or 16 years of working and saving very hard might just be enough for a comfortable retirement. My mother did have a point when she encouraged me to go to work. If I did so, I might only need to continue for 6 more years before I retire forever. However, that assumes that I was not autistic, of course...

Loans to friends

In Secondary school, I saw a business deal went bad. I have done some computer repairs for a friend from another class. I also passed him some computer parts. He promised to pay me for both "soon". I was sensible enough to take his computer as security. He did not pay, so I did not gave him back his computer. However, he had the audacity to make a din outside my apartment to demand his computer back. Unable to out-talk him, I explained the situation to my mother so that she could defeat his aggressive verbal attacks and chase him away. Unwilling to give up, he went to the police station. However, this was a matter for the small claims court and the police will not intervene. Fortunately, his mother intervened and paid me back most of the money. I returned the computer and we never spoke to each other again.

I met an autistic youth who mentioned that he lent money to his friends in school, who tended to continue borrowing from him without repayment.

Fortunately, someone advised him to use this policy: "*If the old debt is unpaid, forget about any new loan*". I had a different answer: "*If you are schooling, never lend money*". That was my policy in school, with the exception of SGD$6.35 that was never paid back. If you are highly unpopular, lending money will not make you popular. Rather, it will become a form of bullying. Even the "no new debt until repayment" policy will induce some smart bully may think, "*Very well, I repay you $1, but I will borrow $100 from you and never return it*".

Friends often assume that you will forgive their debt for small sums and get upset that you still expect repayment. "*What! You still want back that 10 cents!*" Certain people will pretend to forget to repay loans, especially if they spend money very freely and have no savings. It is easier to assume that they are asking for a gift, not a loan. If you lend them money, you must be prepared never to see your money again.

However, in the adult world it may be hard to make friends or please colleagues if you refuse to lend them money. If you must lend, I suggest the following policy:
1. Lend only what you are prepared to give away to the borrower.
2. Never lend the same borrower more than once, unless he has repaid all debts for a few months already.
3. Set a deadline for repayment as early as possible – it is likely that you may be asked to give 1 or 2 extensions.
4. Charge interest for extensions; Even the threat of charging interest might induce early repayment.
5. If possible, obtain something of value as security, which you will return upon repayment or sell upon non-payment.
6. Keep your lending secret, or else you may attract those keen to exploit you.

Frauds & Dubious Schemes
We may be our worst enemy when it comes to protecting our money. Especially when we are in a foreign country or when we are pressured by a fast-talking salesperson, we may relax our financial constrains and goals. I noticed that I tend to be penny wise but pound-foolish: I saved

---

much money from my living expenses but end up losing large sums of money due to bad decisions or fraud.

In 2006, when I first went to China for shopping, I was very generous with my money because the prices there looked like great bargains compared with Singapore. I even gave small tips, which I have never done before. When I met a new Filipino friend in crisis after being conned of his life savings, I gave him a generous amount plus a few gifts. However, after a while reality set in and I cramped down very tightly on my spending.

Some friends tried to recruit me into their "passive income affiliate network", which reminded me of pyramid schemes. I was supposed to recruit other people and obtain passive income via a commission of all the sales they make. I never trust these "get rich quick" ideas, especially if they require expensive membership fees or a hefty investment. I suspect that only those who join the network very early or are talented salespeople will earn money. Knowing that I belonged to neither category, I stayed clear of these "opportunities". I also knew that goods involved may be dubious or marked up at a very high price so that such generous commissions are possible.

A surprising number of people will cheat and betray friends for money. I have heard many stories of how deep relationships lasting decades can evaporate overnight over a few thousand dollars. Some people are ruthless enough to cheat knowing that the victim may be forced sell their only home or borrow money from loan sharks at exorbitant interest rates. I have witnessed this first-hand.

I made a policy never to lend money to strangers because they are often cheats. If you lend them money, you must be prepared to give it away. In Macau, I have lent some money on two separate occasions to strangers who claimed to be in trouble and whom emphasized that they will return the money the next day. Both broke their promise. Nowadays, I ignored them. For beggars, it may be better to donate a loaf of bread instead of money just in case they are fraudulent. To add to my experience, I have also been a victim of pickpockets and counterfeit money.

All these experiences gave me a deeper appreciation of the human condition, showing me the perils of life of Planet Earth. I consoled myself that if I must learn from losing money, then I would rather lose money now when I have little to lose than when I have a lot to lose.

Financial Dependency

On Planet Earth, the act of taking money or help from people without a contract or loan often means that we will have to return a favor to them. If we take large amounts, then we may have to comply with their demands or follow their whims and fancies. This is true even if they are helping us "unconditionally".

I advise others to be wary of accepting money or help that comes with "strings attached". It is best to clarify the relationship before one feels trapped by obligations. The ideal situation is an independent win-win partnership with which both parties benefit each other. As a wise friend advised me, "*We can all be good friends if we don't create expectations and reliance on each other*".

Conclusion

During my childhood, my mother liked to quote a Chinese idiom (人在江湖，身不由己), which roughly translates as "*in the real world, your freedom is constrained.*" Today, I have a deeper appreciation of my mother's social wisdom. On Planet Earth, people often regulate each other's behavior with money. How well we master this "money game" will determine if others control us or if we are in control of our life.

C11: EMPLOYMENT (some advice for autistics)

Work is not a simple process of going to the office, pressing keys on the computer and then collecting a paycheck at the end of the month. I used to think that because I was smart in computers or technical skills, then people must hire me. However, not only did it fail to help me find employment, it gave other people the impression that I was arrogant.

In this chapter, I will share a few simple ground rules about being hired based on my understanding about employment in general. There are 4 "work requirements" we need to perform:
1.   Do what must be done but which your boss prefers not to do, or cannot do
2.   Let your boss feel that you contribute through your work more what than he (or she) pays you
3.   Never threaten your boss' interests or authority
4.   Impress your boss' superiors by showing that he does the above 3 things

Going down to the basics, a job is a trade, not a human rights debate. You trade your time and skills to do what your boss cannot or do not wish to do. In exchange, your boss compensates you with a certain salary. [Of course, a job can be more meaningful than just these economic or political concerns. However, I am simplifying the situation to correct the peculiar ideas that autistics like me have about jobs.]

Job Choices

It is saddening for me to write this. However, I believe that many autistics are unemployable because the non-autistic workplace does not fit well with the autistic working style and attitude. Employers tend to discriminate against those with special needs for good reason. Potential executive planning problems, social problems, attitude problems (such as insubordination, apparent "inattention" and intolerance for interruption) all factor into their decision.

Being a cashier or waiter is likely to be an autistic's nightmare. Being a manager or supervisor is also problematic. The most difficult jobs require autistics to:
- have intensive social interaction
- constantly handle unpredictable changes quickly yet accurately
- listen to verbal instructions that will not be repeated
- perform fine motor movements
- work in a noisy and busy environment

I believe that a good job highlights the strengths and avoids the weaknesses of a person. Instead of going by "*special needs autistic desperate to take a job, asks for reasonable pay and for understanding of other staff*", try "*genius computer programmer who can program in 10 languages, does not need coffee breaks, does not like to waste time chit-chatting with colleagues, specializes in making water-tight code with great security and few bugs*".

Autistics tend to be good with details and systems thinking. They often insist on high quality and tend to work for many hours without rest. Suitable jobs take advantage of their autistic traits and provide:
- Minimum social interaction
- A calm and quiet environment
- Repetitive, predictable chores
- Time to think through problems
- Clearly defined written instructions
- Good use of their favorite interests

Examples of suitable jobs include professors, computer programmer, computer technicians, quality control inspectors, data entry clerks, chemical analysts, lighthouse operators and librarians.

Getting a foothold in the office

An autistic's career may be over within a week if he cannot establish himself as a useful, hardworking and nice person that everyone comes to ask for help. After that, it may be too late to be accepted.

To gain acceptance, non-autistics may make friends with colleagues on the first day of work, treat them to lunch and ally themselves with a small group of like-minded colleagues for protection. Unfortunately, autistics are likely to fail when using such strategies because they cannot grasp the process of social exchange. I suggest the following for autistics to get started in their new job:

1. Choose "pleasant jobs", meaning jobs that make you well-liked and pleasant in the eyes of others. For instance, in an office full of computer illiterate people, the job of a computer technician is highly "pleasant". Avoid "unpleasant" jobs where you give work or make demands for people, like being a supervisor. The down side is that you will be flooded with work, but I believe that this is something you can more easily manage than social rejection.

2. Choose the workplace environment carefully to find one that is safest. Will you have to deal with gangsters and potentially difficult people (such as if you work next to pubs where they hang out)? Do your colleagues expect you to go for expensive social outings with them? How common are incidents of bullying in the type of workplace and industry you are joining? Is your workplace noisy, crowded and chaotic?

3. Get someone you know to put you through the back door of the job, based on your talents and abilities. If you do not have any talent, examine yourself closely to find one now. Otherwise, you may not stand any chance in a formal interview because you look, speak or behave too oddly.

4. Once you get the job, plan carefully about how you can be useful to your colleagues and superiors. Center your strategy on being useful as possible. Avoid creating any trouble or inconvenience for others and do your best to be reliable and consistent in your work. Do not worry too much about your own interests and rights initially. Once you have a good reputation, you can bank on it and get privileges occasionally.

5. On your first day, keep a lookout for friendly and nice colleagues among your immediate workplace, especially those with a higher rank. Carefully choose one of them to be your closest ally and a few to be your general allies. Avoid choosing those of a different branch (or

worse, different department) until you have developed stable "local support". Remember their names and faces: you will be focusing almost all your limited social energies and effort on these people. In time to come, you will rely on them to guide you in your work and navigate any dangerous office politics that you will encounter.

6. Pay attention and observe what irritates and disturbs your allies most. Do not wait for them to ask! Go and offer to help them solve their problems (but be careful not to overdo it)! You have a few days to demonstrate that you are essential to office operations. Of course, do help other people who need help, but spend most of your effort on your allies. Remember: Every time you help someone, no matter how insignificant, you are making a gift to that person.

7. Over the first few days of work, collect intelligence on what equipment is lacking in your office. Find something cheap but presentable and very useful to buy for a selected few who you have chosen as allies. Preferably, each person should receive different gifts (to show that you put in the effort in choosing gifts). It is best for them to think that the gifts cost about the same money so as not to show favoritism. However, check with someone trusted before buying gifts or you could inadvertently violate some unspoken rule and give the wrong kinds of things!

8. If you survived for a few weeks without trouble, then it is time to spread your influence. Observe who has the greatest influence over your destiny and start from the lower ranks. Do not underestimate the accounts clerk who approves your payroll and the HR assistant who types your leave – you will need them if anything goes wrong. Continue your previous strategy of giving useful presents and help.

9. Over the months, work your way slowly up to the supervisors and their bosses. Learn about their pet projects and see what you can offer to make their desires happen. Most importantly, make sure that they hear about your contributions and how much effort you put into helping them. At this moment, you may ask your allies for advice if you feel that you have earned their trust.

10. You must never threaten anyone in the organization. This means that you should not put people out of their job or make them look like they are less intelligent than yourself. Accept praise with openness yet also reserve credit for your allies. Speak about the contributions of

those who may feel threatened by your talent or skills. You must also respect procedures that everyone follows in order to be fair to your colleagues. To avoid giving trouble, you must follow the unspoken customs, not standard official policy. Always observe carefully what your colleagues are doing.

11. If you are given a promotion, consider if the responsibilities will be in harmony with your strategy of "being useful and pleasant". If so, accept it graciously. If not, perhaps you can counter-propose a more suitable job with the suggestion that "you feel that you can contribute more in this way". You can also ask for some time to think about it. After a while, quietly consult with your allies about what the new responsibilities will entail and how to proceed. Prepare to be amazed about their insider knowledge concerning your new job.

12. No matter how highly you are promoted, you can never take your reputation for granted. Always work on your allies and remain pleasant and useful to all people. If you ever lose the support of your subordinates, they may sabotage you to get you fired or demoted. Never underestimate office politics!

Note: It is generally bad taste to tell your colleagues about this plan until they clearly like and trust you. They may think that you are manipulating them and cause the plan to backfire. Keep this to yourself for your own protection.

Staying Hired

Working in your job is not that simple. With today's cost cutting environment, you may have to do the work of 2 or more people. Figure out what will help your allies and immediate superiors most and focus on your efforts accordingly. Do enough work but also rest enough to remain alert.

If you work too fast and finish your job very early, you may consider lying that you have not finished with your first job so that you can attend to another very pressing task. Otherwise, you will never finish working and your boss will blame you for being unreliable or slow. I discovered this terrible irony the hard way.

Remember that you are hired to help your boss do work that he does not want to spend effort on or that he cannot do. Depending on the situation, your boss may want a website he cannot make or to buy lunch without having to queue up. Hence, you shall do these duties for your boss and do it the way that he or she likes. This may be the only point that he will tell you explicitly.

You remain hired if your boss feels that you are giving him enough value for money. Otherwise, he will find someone "cheaper". It is not just how much salary you take but also how much "trouble" you give in return for doing work. If your boss has to pester you every hour because you cannot be bothered to do his pet project or if you pester him with a truckload of questions every time he asks you to do something, you will only last until he finds your replacement.

Demonstrate your value, effort and commitment: Find opportunities to remind your boss subtly of how much contribution you make. (e.g. If you stayed back to work very late, send your boss an email as late as possible so that he knows that you left work late.) If you do not do these, no one will ever know your sacrifices, let alone value you. However, avoid showing off and proclaiming your sacrifices or other people may think that you are complaining about your working conditions.

Do note that every boss has his nemesis: his superior, which may be his supervisor, a board of directors, or the customers he serves. You should present yourself as useful, hardworking and intelligent only to the extent that you do not make him look worse than you do. If you are so much better than your boss, he may worry about you taking over his position. This presents him with a serious dilemma. Some bosses are generous enough to accept competition, but most will tend to feel that you are too arrogant and conceited. Even if they are not desperate enough to sabotage you, they may assign you a lot of work and try their best to make your work life difficult so that you will quit.

By the way, you need not bother pulling an all-nighter researching numbers for a business report, if the report is really about your boss telling his bosses (or customers) that he is a good subordinate. Most boring business meetings make no sense unless you see them as helping your boss demonstrate the 4 "work requirements" to his boss. Help him make that impression and he will be happy with you. You will also receive the bonus of having shorter and happier meetings.

Hence, being employable means that you must demonstrate work ethic.
- **Be obedient**: Give your boss what he wants or better
- **Be reliable**: Check your work carefully and finish it well
- **Be conscientious**: Finish what you started and do it on time
- **Be proactive**: Don't bother your boss if you can solve the problem yourself
- **Be diplomatic**: Maintain good relations for yourself and your boss

Autistic Bosses

When I became aware of the concept of employers and employees, I had a different idea from most people. I wanted to be the employer who makes the decisions and asserts his weight. Thus, when I must serve in the Army as the lowest ranking staff, it was a bitter pill to swallow. However, even if someone made me the boss at that time, I would probably have failed to manage.

I knew an autistic boss (from a wealth family) whose unusual behavior spooked his staff. His inconsistent body language made his staff agitated because they could not read his intentions. His lack of warmth and a friendly attitude made him appear distant and forbidding. His speech tone often roared up and down in mid conversation. His strange laughter did not endear him to others.

To make matters worse, he tended to use insulting language unknowingly. For instance, he would say, "*Why must it have a Chinese design? Why are you so egocentric?*" His reply to a suggestion on improving the contrast of colors on a web page was, "*Are you blind or something? I can see these words very clearly on this brown background.*"

His subordinates confided in me that they want to quit as soon as possible. One was even concerned about potential sexual harassment because she sometimes worked alone in the office with him. People left, people joined, people left. This autistic boss did not know how to make his subordinates comfortable and to let them feel that they are all part of the same team. His only strategy was to treat everyone to lunch or dinner very often.

I believe that his fatal weakness was his business skills. He had a rigidly defined idea of how to run his business and stuck to it despite major changes in his industry. He rented too much office space and could not service the rent. He purchased so many domain names (each with a hefty annual fee) that the receipts filled the entire storeroom from the floor to the ceiling, yet he did not know how to profit from them. He did not know how to please his business partners and seek new clients, so when his most important client fell out with him, his revenue also vanished. The last I heard of him was that he fired his last remaining staff and moved his office into his home.

Conclusion

I believe that it is best for high functioning autistics to:
1. Be hired in a suitable job
2. Do a freelance business that requires minimum social interaction, such as stock trading or website design
3. Avoid starting any major enterprise unless they have the support of a committed team of experienced and capable partners. Even then, it is best for autistics to focus solely on technical operations.

C12: GROWING UP

Planet Earth seemed so terrible and irrational. Why do people constantly misunderstand me? Why is it so hard for the world to agree to stop killing each other? How can some people throw abalone away while others have to eat tree bark? Although I searched in vain for answers to understand Humanity, no one told me that my inner world creates my outer world.

If I could not feel love within me, how could I see it outside? If I do not forgive, how could I find forgiveness? If I felt empty and lonely within, how can someone else fill the void for me? If I do not shed the same tears, how could I comfort other people? If I did not take on Humanity's suffering, how can I deliver Humanity from it? I began to realize that in my quest to solve the puzzle of Humanity, I was taking on the experiences of typical human beings, though in not so typical situations.

As part of the process of becoming human, I experienced the entire range of human emotions - Love, hatred, fear, confidence, anger, achievement, sadness, joy, jealousy, compassion, stress, bliss, lust, satisfaction, loneliness, comfort. However, I refuse to suppress my emotions. I do not like to lie, even if it would make me look bad in front of other people. How can I jeopardize my real mission for something as transient as public reputation?

For instance, I was angry with my mother for her opposition to my work and some of her attitude towards me. Yet, I was also grateful for her help and upbringing. Unfortunately, my anger often overwhelmed my gratefulness. To most people, it was "wrong" for me to feel this way, but it was even more wrong for me to lie by forcing myself to feel something I did not feel.

For the past months while I was writing this book, my mother has made it clear that I should give up on my autism work because it does not pay enough to support the family. Many people agreed with her, saying that I was stubborn, unrealistic and immature. I disagreed. I believed that my work might change the evolution of autism research. How many people in the world had experiences like mine? How many are willing to put themselves under public scrutiny? Was it wrong for me to put the world ahead of my family? Nah, it was more important to get a job now before I grow old and unemployable. It was more important to earn a few thousand dollars a month to bunker up for a rainy day than to aspire to change the world.

I could not accept that argument, until my mother begged me. "*I have let you try so many times, and what have you achieved? I have listened to you so many times, so why can't you just listen to me just this time?*" What can I say? Can I bear to turn her down again as a son? Will I set a good example for other autistics if I ignored her again?

I felt that I had lost my ideals on that night when my mother cried. Too bad I did not have the financial freedom afforded by a wealthy family. Too bad my book deals and plans all never worked out. The tough decisions and painful failures I encountered showed me the harsh reality on this primitive planet, where most people trade in their ideals for job security.

It was painful, but I grew up that night and found my answer about how to understand Humanity. Everyone, autistic or not, arrives at maturity by walking the painful path of experience. Since I must walk this path, I will find a job and work just like my peers. I can only wonder how many of us will choose to treat our experiences as our allies rather than our enemies?

Why grow up?

When we are young children, it is OK to say things like "*when I grow up, I will be a scientist who will end world hunger*". Or even, "*when I grow up, I will be an astronaut who will put the Chinese flag on the moon*". People say that it is good for children to dream. But the problem starts when we really grow up...

1. **Money**: The number one challenge for most Earthlings is to get enough of money so that they can survive. It is difficult to accomplish anything important on Planet Earth without money. Although we can ask someone else to help us, people who provide

money often tend to control and restrict what we do, making it difficult to accomplish our goals. It is better to have our own money so that we can do what we like.

2. **Job**: A job requires us to do something that someone else wants us to do in return for money. A job is usually the only way we can get money, unless we win millions in a lottery, inherit a large fortune or marry a rich partner. Unfortunately, it may be hard to find a job that pays enough money. Jobs usually require pieces of paper called certificates, which we spend much money and time to obtain. We must obtain it even if what we do to get the paper has nothing to do with doing our job. Without the paper, people may not hire us even if we are talented and capable.

3. **Taxes**: When we do get a job, we have to give money to our government, which is the agency that Earthlings have created to keep themselves under control. Some governments take more than half our salary to do nasty things like killing people with bombs. Despite moral objections, we must pay up unless we give up our freedom to live in heavily guarded government hotels called jails.

4. **Family**: After we pay the government, we need to pay our family, which is another Earthling invention to help their race survive and propagate. Having a family is one of the biggest reasons why most Earthlings dare not quit their job – their family may not survive if they have no money.

5. **Ourselves**: We may need to provide not only our body's basic needs, but also for transport, clothing and other expenses needed to blend in with other Earthlings around us. To add to our burden, we may have acquired certain customs or habits that require much money to feed, such as gambling, drinking alcohol and smoking.

6. **Friends**: Most Earthlings have friends that they like to spend time being together. Friends make life more interesting and meaningful for them. Facilitating friendship requires not only good social skills, but also food and gifts. If they have any money leftover from taxes, family contributions and our expenses, they often spend them on friends.

For the sake of simplicity, let us assume that if we have understood, experienced and can handle the above 6 key issues, then we can be considered grown-up. If we use this standard of comparison, then many autistics are not mature yet. A mother wrote me a heart wrenching email about how her 25-year-old son refused to find a job and spends all his time in a virtual world called "Second Life". She asked, *"What can I do to help him return to the real world?"*

Uh-oh. There are no money, jobs, taxes, families, human bodies and friends on Planet Asperger. Instead, there are idealists, volunteers, recognition, libraries, computers and interesting projects. By Earth standards, Planet Asperger's inhabitants have it easy. In contrast, Planet Earth is a horrific, painful and soul-wrenching place.

I wonder how many inhabitants of Planet Asperger would like to give up on their ideals and pet projects in exchange for doing meaningless work and compromising their goals for irrational social demands. How many of them are keen to migrate to Planet Earth knowing that:

1. Every day, almost 16,000 children die from hunger while bakeries and restaurants routinely throw perfectly good food away.
2. The richest 225 people have more money than 3 billion of the world's poor. While the rich are flying in their corporate jets, the poor are staving to death.
3. The cost of one missile can provide lunch for a school of hungry children everyday for 5 years. However, certain people prefer to use that missile to kill a school of hungry children instead.
4. The wealthy nations spend $60 billion on programs to assist the poorest nations but *$900 billion* on defense. Guns and bombs are apparently more important than food and medical care.

Many Earthlings tell me that these facts are irrelevant. Find a job, fill my stomach, then worry about such things 40 years later after I retire. That was supposed to be the mature thing to do, isn't it? I would like to ask these people if the following practices encourage migration to Planet Earth:

1. Covering up fellow Earthlings' faults with unclear, emotionally laden justifications
2. Repetitively advertising the most undesirable features of Planet Earth to potential migrants
3. Sweeping potential migrant protests and objections under the carpet instead of letting skilled diplomats clarify the situation
4. Refusing to recognize the lifestyle on Planet Asperger as equally valid to lifestyles on Planet Earth
5. Requiring potential migrants to abandon their old lifestyle and take on a completely alien new lifestyle instead of integrating both lifestyles
6. Treating potential migrants as incapable of deciding what to do with their life
7. Constantly harassing potential migrants who refuse to migrate

I do not think I can pass judgment on either party and say who is at fault. I can only hope for my work to help bring awareness to the people of both worlds about their misunderstandings, so that they may soon find ways to accept each other.

Experiential Maturity

What does it mean to carry ourselves confidently? What does it mean to grow up and become mature? What does it mean to find a job and a life partner? Most of us probably need not think twice about these ineffable answers, but for me, I have to discover the answers consciously.

When desires awaken in me, I sought physical contact and companionship. When I saw that opening car doors, helping to serve drinks and being "gentlemanly" pleased other people, I wanted to continue. When a part of me saw my failures as temporary, I stopped my complaining and walked with confidence. When a flash of thought flickered through my mind while my mother nagged me, I knew why a job is so important. When I felt the pain of giving up my ideals in order to provide for my family, I can relate to the billions who must have had such experiences.

I can define maturity by the experiential understanding of the concepts below:

1. **Humble Perspective**: We see ourselves as a tiny part of the big picture, each with our individual lives to live. I used to have great difficulty accepting that other people have their own set of troubles, problems and prejudices. As a result, I placed excessive demands on people without knowing it and gave the impression of arrogance.

   Society is like a huge organism that consists of individuals like us. It has tradition, rules and existing systems to maintain its stability. Understanding this gave me respect for the creations of Earthlings, and the ingenuity and sacrifices people before me had made to create what I experience today.

2. **Confronting Suffering**: As an adult, we experience the ugly, mundane and imperfect in our lives. They include ill-mannered bosses, jealous colleagues, unreliable partners and various forms of dishonesty. They come with serious implications: flunking exams is nothing compared to being bankrupt and out of a job with a family to feed. When we choose to accept these, we take a big step towards maturity.

3. **Impermanence**: Our humble perspective expands to time, and we see our troubles as temporary and minor in the cosmic scheme of things.

4. **Behavior**: When we experience and understand what other people have gone through, we start to regulate our emotional responses and reactions, causing our behavior to follow. Empathy and respect arises.

5. **Practical Plans**: Refining our plans through experience, our emotional instinct and mental understanding, we create plans that are simple, coherent and self-correcting. Focusing solely on logic and efficiency, I often thought of unnecessarily complex plans that require important events to happen the way I have planned in order to work. As a result, people disliked working with me.

Mature Attitude

I believe that if we have a mature perspective, we would have a mature attitude. To me, a mature attitude consists of:

1. **Accepting Sacrifices**: We make painful choices in our lives while fully aware of the likely consequences of our actions in the future. We must accept and live with our past decisions.
2. **Confidence**: Both failures and success are like passing clouds – they do not stay for long. By contrast, our confidence shines like the sun, knowing that we are only doing our work on this world.
3. **Empathy**: The lives of other people are revealed through our own lives, their thoughts through our own thoughts, their emotions through our own emotions. We treat people the way we wish others to treat us.
4. **Respect**: The culture, inventions and systems that people have created serve their roles, even if they are inefficient and imperfect. We honor the ways of the ancients while accepting innovation.
5. **Cohesion**: We lead by following. We do not demand that the other take the first step in finding a balance with us. Rather, we step into balance with the other first.

C13: DEVELOPING CREATIVITY

During my childhood, I could not do anything about myself because I was not truly awake. After I awoke, creativity, self-awareness and a proactive attitude were the essential ingredients that laid my foundation for leaving autism's limitations.

Personality Split

I came from a Mandarin speaking family. Around Primary 3, I started developing a split personality within myself, after years of exposure to English books. My English self arose that contained the intelligent, studious and talkative parts of me. The other parts of me remained with the Mandarin self, which tended to be non-verbal, unresponsive and unthinking.

My English self was active in school. I could relate to other teachers like an adult. Thinking in English, I have access to analytical abilities and problem solving skills that I did not develop previously. However, my Mother did not understand English, and so my Mandarin self struggled to communicate with her. Eventually, I developed a strategy of letting my English self handle the thinking while Mandarin self performed the translation. This only introduced a 1 to 2 second delay in my response, which was a significant improvement for me.

By the end of 2005, my English self has made great leaps in its language abilities and innate understanding of concepts. However, my Mandarin self was only able to handle routine conversations. Abstract topics or less common concepts required internal translation. This system stayed with me until around the end of 2006. Frequently having to share my experiences and abstract thoughts in Mandarin, I decided to improve my ability to think natively in Mandarin.

I believed that splitting my personality allowed the most functional parts of my mind to develop independently from the less functional parts. This might have helped me focus on developing these more functional parts to their full potential.

Developing a Sense of Self

In December 1996, I went to one of the national library branches to obtain more reading material. Usually I spend my time in the science section, but this time I wandered around. I borrowed a psychology textbook that caught my eye. In about 2 weeks, I read all 600 pages, summarized the main points and printed these on 3 pages of paper. That began my exploration of psychology and self help.

A few months later, my male classmate Kelly introduced me to a book entitled "The Einstein Factor". This book showed me the concept that I had more potential than I thought I have and there are ways to unlock these potential. Kelly only read up to page 32, but I finished it. I continued to read more related books such as "Superlearning 2000". They told me to take control of my future, develop new perspectives and break both tradition and norm with creative thinking.

As I treated what I read as Absolute Truth, I obeyed their commands and decided to spread the Gospel. Over the next few months, I went on a one-boy campaign to revolutionize the educational system. My teachers were not impressed but made some effort to humor me. They told me that while some of the concepts would be useful in adult life, they are all outside the syllabus and thus irrelevant. Although I was socially inept, I cannot help but notice that my teachers are not interested to listen to me and apply my ideas. As this struck me, I realized that I must choose to either return to my old self by forgetting about everything or live a different life following my new discoveries. Since my teachers or parents did not support this new adventure, I would have to disobey them.

This may perhaps be the first conscious, life-altering decision that I made. This choice awakened me from my sleepwalking state and drew a line between "Self" and "Other". It began the journey to develop independent thought instead of accepting what I read in books or heard from authority figures.

Unofficial Role Model

My Secondary school classmate Kelly not only introduced me to self-improvement works but also guided me with his example. A self-made leader, he had a proactive attitude. Whenever he encountered an obstacle, he would utter his trademark statement: "Improvise..."

To me, Kelly represented independence, creativity and taking action. Incapable of and unwilling to learn from others, I had to improvise everything in my Life. In the past, when I encountered a new problem, I might freeze in panic and wait for rescue. After I modeled Kelly, I analyzed the situation, recalled what I have learnt from my reading and devised a new solution to solve the problem. I strode into the Brave New World with full mental confidence.

Developing my first Life Mission

After spending months considering what to do with my life, I decided to create a massive Scientific Research Institution that will hire the world's best scientists to solve all the world's problems. To fund this project, I estimated that I needed US$10 billion dollars. "*No problem*", I thought, "*by age 35 I will get it done*". When I told some people around me about my dreams, they reacted along the lines of "*what a ridiculous idea!*" They denounced my dream as unrealistic and impractical without giving logically convincing reasons. They were only keen to deny me, deny my dreams; deny all of what I stood for.

I found that I had to defend myself against this onslaught of negativity and discouragement – a verbal war that I could never win. I felt that it was unfair for me to carry the burden of proof alone. Unwilling to deny myself of my truth, I rejected them and did my best to make sure that they were wrong and I right. I sought to improve myself as much as I could. I read the business section of the newspaper, tuned in to the news channel before going to school and monitored the global stock markets. I also tried to sign up for a free stock investment seminar advertised in the newspaper. The phone receptionist must have guessed my age from my voice because he told me to "*go to school and study hard*".

Other than creating my own education and trying to do business, my attitude of taking charge of my life extended to my family as well. When my parents were on the verge of a divorce, I decided to call a Government counseling centre and booked an appointment for both of them. The appointment was a dismal failure, but the counselor was impressed and thought that I was rather mature.

Making sense of the world

While I had some exciting adventures outside, I had an even busier inner life. I intuitively recognized that all knowledge is interconnected. I studied subjects like biology, finance or philosophy without considering them as separate fields of knowledge. For instance, the flow of water can also explain the flow of electricity. The evolution of businesses has similarities with the evolution of living things in nature. The supposedly subjective beliefs we have may influence reality via quantum physics. I constantly sought to connect what I studied with each other in a meaningful manner.

Although I did not know how I did that, I was aware of my knowledge coming together in a beautiful multi-dimensional crystal-like "building". The symbols and links within this building gave me access to lateral thinking and creativity: whenever I thought of something, I received a few related thoughts that may cut across many subjects.

I treated my mind like a computer. Sometimes I entered commands into it with strange symbols that I could not see clearly, moving my hand physically as if typing them on a keyboard. As my mind processed the information, windows of symbols would open and close while data lines ran across my mindscape. Symbol structures would rotate, transform and realign. Multi-dimensional shapes attempted to fit together with each other. I was unaware that other people did not think in this way.

My Issues

1. **False Confidence**: As explained earlier

2. **Unrealistic Expectations**: I wanted everything to happen perfectly and anything less is a failure.

3. **Unsystematic Exploration**: I did not do my due diligence. The estimates for my plans came from my imagination, not real world conditions. Sometimes, I took on an idea because I read about it in a book, rather than consider its chances of success, realistic profits and growth potential.

   If my new idea failed, I quickly abandoned it and tried another. I adapted this strategy from the story of Thomas Edison experimenting with many wrong materials before finding one that worked for his light bulb. I imagined that there are infinite ideas, and if I searched enough ideas, I might hit one that worked. I did not realize how much more complex the problems of Planet Earth are compared to a light bulb.

4. **Only Textbook Understanding**: I relied mostly on books to guide me. I did not notice my handicaps in social skills and executive planning.

C14: CREATING MENTAL INTERFACES

Some of the Self Improvement books introduced me to NLP (Neuro-Linguistic Programming) which contains techniques for reprogramming our subconscious. Among many things, it can remove phobias, foster higher self-esteem (e.g. believing that one is capable of scoring well in school) and enhance creativity. [Note: NLP is not designed for use by autistics in general and does not cure autism.]

Unfortunately, I had only a superficial understanding of NLP and became obsessed with it. Fortunately, a sensible part-time history teacher scolded me, punching holes in my peculiar ideas of what NLP can do. Although I felt the most revolting feelings, I stood still and listened. Afterwards, my obsession with NLP ended completely. In time to come, what I read about NLP and psychology helped me create my own derivative techniques for coping with autism.

Looking back, I hypothesize that many parts of my brain were not functioning properly, especially those that rely on emotions. I unknowingly used NLP-like mental interfaces to reroute the brain functions through other circuits that work. For example, my visual, verbal, logical, pattern detection and lateral thinking circuits still functioned well. In addition, I had deeper access to my subconscious than most people. I could sometimes track my thoughts step by step as they arise. I also could also create mental interfaces whenever I needed them.

Paying Attention in Class

During my rebellion, I started reading science, psychology, Self Improvement, business and various books in class. I took care to hide them behind the school textbook or under the table. Some teachers started noticing that I did pay attention to their lessons. They would check on me by asking me to stand up and repeat what they just said.

I noticed that my mind has a function that fades out audio sensory impressions quickly. Apparently, this buffer allows my mind to understand audio speech. By modifying it to improve the strength of the buffer, I devised an audio loop program to record the last 3 to 5 seconds of all speech I hear. To make this system, I imagined a doughnut shaped container with a moving line intersecting part of it. As my ears picked up raw speech, the moving line "impressed" them into the container, overwriting any previous content. When there is a need to repeat the words, I stop and reset the line into play mode. As the line passed over the rest of the doughnut, I let the raw speech run from my mouth. The catch is that I must divert 10% of my attention to the recording process. The other 90% remained for me to use to read my book. My teachers never found out.

Dancing Program

My Secondary school organized a special enrichment workshop called Camp Discovery for the students. One of the highlights was an event where we dance to music without following any steps. My classmates "volunteered" me and I went along. I thought for a while about how to dance and figured out that I could simply randomize my body movement. I quickly made a little program to feed random instructions to my body. As I saw moving cylinders and symbols in my mind, my body followed these and went by "random instinct".

It was a success. People asked me where I got my dance moves. I replied that I had no idea. Someone commented that I had some Michael Jackson moves. However, I never watched MTV and had no interest at all in dancing. In the Polytechnic, I did a repeat performance for some teammates at a group project. I later helped to train some performers on another derivative of this dancing style for my friend's amateur theatre project in 2005.

Face Recognizer

As my face-recognition instinct did not work, it was as difficult to distinguish human faces from each other as the faces of sheep of the same size and species. While in Polytechnic, I installed a program in my mind that computed how likely the face I am looking at is someone I know and display the results as a digital percentage. If the probability is higher than 80%, I would greet and wave to the person. Otherwise, I would pretend not to notice the person just in case this is a false negative. The system worked well most of the time.

Navigation Guidance System

I found it troublesome to think about how to walk, so around the 2001, I devised my own navigation guidance system. I had my mind overlay a system of arrows, lines and dots to guide me on my surroundings. I only needed to follow the direction of the arrows and note the lines in front of me indicating if I should speed up or slow down. This made routine walks much more interesting.

When there is a crowd of people that I must pass through, the guidance system would draw a red line indicating a recommended passage. It would also present me with a 2-dimensional screen tracking all people in my visual awareness. When I cross roads without the aid of traffic lights, the system would track all incoming vehicles and calculate the next available window for me to cross safely. It would also conveniently count down the seconds for me.

My navigation system could also display a map, track my present location and display telemetry such as my estimated walking speed. I used units called "Wrap", where "Wrap 1" is the most people's normal walking speed. I tend to walk at "Wrap 3.5". This term was inspired by Star Trek – I liked to think of myself as a spaceship traveling through outer space. Nowadays, I measure speed in terms of "engine load". I set engines at 10% load on leisure walks with other people or 80% load during normal walking. If I were in a terrible rush, I push my engines to redline, giving me the maximum walking speed possible. When this happens, the navigation system would issue a warning and count down to engine failure.

Body Control System

Around 1999, in order to improve my fine-motor skills, I visualized simplified versions of my body parts and tracked these in 3-dimensional space. For instance, a thick line would represent my hand and five smaller lines my fingers. The system would also issue instructions on using how much force to exert and what direction to move my hand. This probably reduced the number of accidents I had. However, it created a heavy strain on my conscious mind when in operation.

C15: FINDING MEANING & TRUST

Unable to derive sensory pleasures, I only experienced the pain, suffering and ugliness of the world around me. I found beauty only in knowledge, logic and systems. I avoided the terrible real world in favor of my beautiful and perfect mental realm. As I matured, I realized that the world around us is also part of us, reflecting our inner world. If it is dirty, that is because our inner world is dirty. If it is sick, that is because our inner world is sick. I had such a negative view of the world because there are parts of me that I could not embrace. Once I accepted them into my life, I accepted the world into me.

I realized that we live within the cycles of life. Through our senses, we breathe the world into ourselves. Through our words and actions, we breathe out into the world. As we breathe in the world, we digest the world into part of ourselves. As we breathe out to the world, the world digests us as part of itself. People who understand the cycle move together with the world, advancing and retreating, acting and resting. The in-breath builds the foundation of the out-breath; the out-breath creates the potential of the in-breath. It is simply so beautiful...

I realized that my impatience does not help me to enjoy the passage of time. I realized that my need for perfection does not help me to digest my life as a human being. I realized that my body is also capable of giving me pleasure and joy. I realized that Planet Earth is not a slow and terrible place, but potentially an exciting and joyful playground. As the realizations slowly dawn on me, I began my process of uniting with my World. I began to accept the fact that I am a human being living on Planet Earth. I began to accept my bodily and mental limitations, and to make the best use of them. I began to accept myself for Who I Am.

I am sharing the most frequently asked questions I would like in 1997, when I secretly wish that a mysterious, wise old man would explain them all to me.

Why are there bureaucratic rules?

I used to dislike bureaucratic rules or guidelines because I thought that they only stopped me from my finishing work as quickly and efficiently as possible. When I served as a clerk in the Singapore Army, one of my superiors used to emphasize that I need to triple check everything I do,

One day, I did not check as thoroughly and left out a name in an internal survey. It was serious: my mistake could skew the survey results and offend the person whose name was missing. I was fearful of the repercussions including potential punishment. Fortunately, my superior took the blame for me. He claimed that he did not review my work so that he had to apologize. Still feeling responsible, I apologized to the person whose name I missed out. Although she did not blame me, unfortunately, but the damage was already done to some of the survey results. After that incident, I never dared to relax my vigilance.

Why do humans do mundane work?

I disliked doing housework and maintenance. I wanted to focus all my time and effort on assimilating knowledge and implementing my plan to change the world. Housework was an unnecessary distraction that only existed because humans were too technologically primitive to automate it fully.

It was only while reading a Zen book that I discovered how work could take on a different dimension. As I scrubbed the toilet bowl, I saw myself scrubbing the impurities in my mind. As I mopped the floor, I saw myself wiping away my inner dirt. Moving back and forth with my instruments, I purified myself.

During my stay in Macau, I saw the social value of work. It is not just play and adventure that brings people together, but who is helping to mop the floor and laying out the dishes. Doing ordinary chores together fosters the team spirit.

Why not just agree on one thing?

Different people have had different experiences and opinions. It was difficult for me to accept the diversity of this world because I could not see the different but equally important roles that other people play in our world. I did not realize how each of us has to make painful choices in order to mature. As we pay the price of making these choices, they define our unique character and destiny.

Walking through the roller-coaster of life proved exciting and eye-opening, especially after I came to Macau and assumed independence from my parents in Singapore. I was praised for my sacrifice and talent. I was cheated of my money. I made people cry both happy tears and sad ones. I made new friends and I embraced new languages and cultures. I rediscovered my racial roots and the Chinese culture.

There were both good things and bad, and many difficult decisions I must make in the face of total uncertainty. As I went through each incident, I understood more and more about life on Planet Earth. This process happens to everyone else too as they grow up. Witnessing the process myself, I could no longer say that I am at the centre of the world anymore. Neither can I say that there is only one answer for everything.

Why do humans use a hierarchy system?

People are prone to tell me that the hierarchical system is the way that the world works. In order to live in society, I must learn to accept my place in this system and the duties that come with it. I, however, could not be satisfied with such explanations. I wanted something more, something logical that my mind could grasp and something more meaningful than blind obedience. Other people did not entertain me on this request. Instead, I found out by myself the hard way.

During my business foray in 2006, my partners often refused to fulfill their duties due to emotional or other vague reasons. However, I lacked the authority to enforce responsibilities or fire them because we did not follow any hierarchy.

In the Army with its many rules and regulations, I realized just how cumbersome and time-consuming democratic decision-making is. When we are in a rush and we know the situation closely, it is much easier to decide right away what to do than to obtain decision from a group of hard to contact people who might not even understand the situation at all.

Earthlings have created a hierarchy system where some people hold more influence and others less. This allows a team of people to finish work quickly. Not only will this reduce the number of people who needed to make decisions to as few as one person (thereby speeding up decision making), everyone has to perform their duties no matter if they are in a good mood or not (thereby creating a reliable schedule for completing work). This is the best that Earthlings could do in their current stage of evolution, where few of them have the maturity to be responsible, reliable and independent. Rather than complain, I should improve myself to be one of those who are mature enough to lead.

How can we forgive those who have hurt us?

During an emotional releasing session, I recalled an incident in Primary 3 when a classmate surrounded me with his friends and started kicking me. I panicked and stood helplessly during the assault. Suddenly, I saw this young gang leader at home. His father arrived reeking of alcohol, started spitting vulgarities and then beat both mother and child. After seeing the young gang leader cry out helplessly in pain, I saw him as a tattoo-laden teenager being arrested by the police. The events started to fast-forward: I saw him being released from jail, only to find himself back inside. This cycle repeated itself a few times, until it stopped with a scene of him gazing out of the prison bars at the moon in the night sky, desperately wishing to be free.

I was crying as I witnessed him unable to step outside his painful past without a future that can inspire him. Although I have no way of finding out if what I saw was true, but I forgave him at that instant. There was no other possible choice, because I just experienced the statement "all attack is a cry for help". Other people hurt us because they are hurt themselves. As I wrote, I remembered a passage in the Bible:

You have heard that it was said, 'An eye for an eye and a tooth for a tooth.' But I tell you not to resist evildoers. On the contrary, whoever slaps you on the right cheek, turn the other to him as well. If anyone wants to sue you and take your shirt, let him have your coat as well. And if anyone forces you to go one mile, go two with him.

Give to the person who asks you for something, and do not turn away from the person who wants to borrow something from you. You have heard that it was said, 'You must love your neighbor' and hate your enemy. But I say to you, love your enemies, and pray for those who persecute you, so that you will become children of your Father in heaven. For he makes his sun rise on the evil and the good, and he lets rain fall on the righteous and the unrighteous.

For if you love those who love you, what reward will you have? Even the tax collectors do the same, don't they? And if you greet only your brothers, what great thing are you doing? Even the Gentiles do the same, don't they? So be perfect, as your heavenly Father is perfect."
(Mat 5:38 to Mat 5:48)

What is human?

Caught up in a spree of book writing in April 2005, I just sat in front of my computer and a stream of words would just flow from me. I wrote three 80-pages A4 sized books every 2 weeks and another book in a month. However, I did not publish them as I deemed their quality insufficient. In the meantime, my emotions were still raw and awakening like a young teenager.

Inspired to write a story, I took a different approach. Instead of taking past stories or my personal events and working out the story events part by part, I defined the environment, the characters and the ending as clearly as possible. I then pressed the "play" button and let the story run. The characters came alive. They had their own independent thoughts, emotions and will. They moved about in the virtual story world, weaving out the story. Relegated to the role of a reporter, I watched their every movement, felt their every emotion and thought their every thought. I recorded all my observations these into a document within my computer. The characters were convincing and the emotions were fresh and vivid, unlike all my past attempts at fiction.

One night, I stopped to take a rest and gazed at passing cars on the road in front of my apartment. As I saw a yellow taxi, a realization hit me. I saw myself in the story of Life. I saw each of us living in the story, playing our roles as we lived. I saw the great weaving of the world that each of us is doing. I felt the Eternal Observer and the Eternal Creator, all at once. I saw how strange concepts like "the Future changing the Past" and "Synchronicity" are routine in Story Time. Many thoughts about the world came to me, drifted by and disappeared. Stunned, I rested in my chair and reminisced about the process of Life, and Story Writing.

I felt it – a glimpse of the human experience. Seeing what I had missed out, I stopped judging human beings as irrational and imperfect. Feeling the contrast between the autistic and non-autistic consciousness also inspired me to write my emotions, thoughts and new insights into my first published book, Mirror Mind.

How can we achieve world peace?

As I continued writing, I saw countless sentient beings existing in my mind. Just like in the real world, they are disagreements, conflicts and alliances. There are the good and evil, weak and the strong, the instinct-driven and objective, the idealistic and the practical-minded. Ruling the entire Inner Kingdom is my Conscious Mind.

Unlike in an autocracy, these mental forces can and often refuse to accept my decision. They quarrel, protest and wreck havoc. The power of the governed is far stronger than the government, capable of rebelling and overthrowing it. The government can maintain its power in a few ways, such as keeping the people divided in weak fractions, using propaganda or convincing the people to support a unified policy built with charisma, wisdom and love.

The real-world governments in our world are great examples of how we rule ourselves. From their examples, I learnt mostly what not to do with my people. I will not force my people to adopt official beliefs over their own. I will not cover up and ignore my people's voices, even if it causes me embarrassment or bad reputation. I will attend to every belief and create a new policy that has a place for all these beliefs. How I deal with my inner beings influences how I deal with other people outside of me. Knowing that I cannot give what I do not have, I must attain peace within myself before I can bring peace to Planet Earth.

How do we accept the unexpected?

While I was in Macau, I encountered many unexpected failures and sudden unpleasant changes of plan. My desire to show results to my mother before my return to Singapore put me under great stress to succeed. The stress and emotional chaos accumulated over the months and became particularly intense when I must rush the first draft of this book for an upcoming print run in Macau weeks before I was ready to deliver the material.

Sensing my distress, a friend told me a story about the 6th Zen Patriarch Hui Neng. The summary of the story went something like this:

> After accepting Hui Neng as his student, the 5th Patriarch sent him to the kitchen to split firewood and pound rice for 8 months. One day, the 5th Patriarch told his monks to express their wisdom in a poem. Whoever had true realization of his original nature (i.e. Buddha Nature) would be ordained the 6th Patriarch. The learned head monk, Shen Hsiu, wrote the following:

> > *The body is the wisdom-tree,*
> > *The mind is a bright mirror in a stand;*
> > *Take care to wipe it all the time,*
> > *And allow no dust to cling.*

> The poem was praised by many people, but The 5th Patriarch knew that Shen Hsiu had not yet found his original nature. Later, Hui Neng heard about the poem and asked someone to write down his poem, which read:

> > *Fundamentally no wisdom-tree exists,*
> > *Nor the stand of a mirror bright.*
> > *Since all is empty from the beginning,*
> > *Where can the dust alight*

Hearing the poem, I suddenly saw in my mind the vast expense of space. I saw endless universes being created and destroyed. I saw that we are only a small speck in the vastness. Suddenly, things no longer mattered to me. A great feeling of comfort held me and I was inspired to recite the Buddhist Heart Sutra:

> *Avalokitesvara Bodhisattva, while doing deep prajna paramita*
> *Saw clearly the emptiness of all 5 conditions*
> *Thus completely relieving misfortune and pain*

O Shariputra, form is no other than emptiness, emptiness no other than form
Form is exactly emptiness, emptiness exactly form
Sensation, conception, discrimination, awareness are likewise this

O Shariputra, all teachings and universal laws are forms of emptiness
Not born, not destroyed
Not stained, not pure
Without gain, without loss

In emptiness, there exists no form, sensation, conception, discrimination or awareness
No eye, ear, nose, tongue, body, mind
No color, sound, smell, taste, touch, phenomena

No realm of sight, no realm of consciousness
No ignorance and no end to ignorance
No ageing and death, and no end to ageing and death
No suffering, and no cause of suffering
No extinguishing, no path

No wisdom and no gain
No gain and thus
The Bodhisattva lives prajna paramita

With no attachment of the mind
No attachment, and thus no fear
Far beyond deluded thoughts
This is (the state of) nirvana

All past, present and future Buddhas live prajna paramita
Therefore attaining all penetrating, perfect enlightenment
Therefore know that prajna paramita is

The great Mantra
The vivid Mantra
The best Mantra
The unsurpassable Mantra

It completely clears all pain
This is the truth
So set forth the Prajna Paramita mantra
Set forth this mantra and say:

Gone! Gone! [Gate, Gate]
Gone beyond! [Paragate]
Gone far beyond! [Parasamgate]
Hail such an awakening! [Bodhi Svaha]

Note:
Prajna = pure awareness without discrimination
Paramita = to cross to the other side

Now that it no longer mattered about what I do, I could let go of all my expectations and demands. I broke into tears and uttered softly: "*Because the vast majority of sentient beings could not understand this, they are trapped in the endless ocean of suffering.*" After my tears stopped, my friend continued, "*I have not finished. Most people believed that this poem demonstrated Hui Neng's understanding of his Original Nature. However, at this time, he still has not fully understood yet.*"

> The Fifth Patriarch pretended that he was not impressed with this poem either, but he arranged to meet with Hui Neng in the middle of the night and conferred with him. When he mentioned a passage from a Buddhist sutra about "being mindful", Hui Neng finally understood.

> The Fifth Patriarch then gave him the insignia of his office, the Patriarch's robe and bowl. He told Hui Neng to leave for the South and hide his enlightenment until the proper time arrives for him to propagate the Dharma.

He finished the story, but I did not understand the last point: "Be mindful". I reflected about this for many minutes. Suddenly, a "library" of people came to my mind. I saw an amalgam of all kinds of people, in all kinds of stories. It was as if, all possible people in all possible existences appeared to me. Then I realized that there is nothing for them to do, except their job. That was Who They Are.

I felt renewed, because I have nothing left but to do my. "*Give unto the people in my life what belongs to them, unto the world what belongs to the world, and unto me what belongs to me.*" I reexamined my situation and noticed that I have already done many things that do not express Who I Am. Although I could not take back my words or actions, my future is waiting for me, and the present is for me to use.

I stepped back into the world with confidence. I did my best with what I could do. Firstly, I made a decision to leave my sponsor and return to Singapore. When the book publishing sponsorship did not materialize, I accepted it and moved on. I tried but failed to negotiate book deals with

2 organizations. When my mother confronted me, I made a painful decision to acknowledge my failures, stop my autism work and follow my mother's wishes to find full-time employment after my remaining commitments in Hong Kong. I could only do so when I am willing to let go of my attachment to my autism work.

Why am I here?

I believed that science could solve every problem Humanity had. After I awakened to self-awareness, I wondered what if I contributed US$10 billion for scientific research. Perhaps Humanity could find a cure for cancer, AIDS and many diseases. Perhaps we could deploy new technologies to reverse the effects of pollution on Planet Earth.

To achieve this target, I set a goal to earn SGD$10 million by age 25 and US$10 billion by age 35. I then asked myself what it would take to achieve this. The first step is to learn about money, science and people. That set my 3-prong strategy to learn about business, science and psychology. I considered everything else in school that did not fit in with my strategy as irrelevant. Although I did not fully understand what I studied, I read about exchange rates, currency inflation, business studies, the banking system and some accountancy. Although I did not know what I was doing, I strove to expose myself to the business world.

However, I felt constantly taxed to my limits. No matter how hard I study, I could not finish all the books I borrowed from the library. I felt that there was simply not enough time, and I must always hurry, hurry and hurry. The stress grew for years until I had a constant burden weighing down on my shoulders. I desperately needed a vacation but I could not give that to myself.

In 2003, I had an answer. As I was about to take a break at home, I closed my eyes and found myself floating in front of a huge space city. Suddenly, I was in front of its metallic looking walls. I touched it. It was paper thin, yet as strong as a thick wall of steel. It was neither cold nor warm, and seemed to have a patterned, scratchproof surface. It did not feel like metal, but a material yet to be invented.

Suddenly, I saw a room with a few scientists working on an incredibly advanced computer system. I saw a model of a Faster Than Light (FTL) spaceship and complex calculations flashing by as the scientists handled the engine design. I then found myself in space, with a huge metallic looking object moving slowly below me. My view moved further away to reveal a massive spaceship, many miles long. I realized that this was Humanity's first prototype ship.

I then found myself in person, facing a conference hall with the delegates from the space cities. To my left was an Asian woman. To her left was a man who seemed to have European features. The room became quiet and the audience attentive. The woman turned to me, and said, "*Now that Humanity is about to make history, would you like to have the honor?*" I replied, "*The honor is yours.*" As she slid the level in front on the podium, and the ship jumped through space and vanished. As the thought of what is happening to the ship arose, a panel of numbers and associated feelings appeared to me indicating its status. I noted that we could communicate with the computer directly, without keyboard and mice.

The delegates murmured as the ship traveled a programmed course around the nearest star system, Alpha Proxima. After more than half an hour, Humanity held its collective breath, waiting for the ship to appear. As it did, the audience burst into wild applause. I also caught a glimpse of all the people in the space cities cheering in joy.

Now I found myself in a park with trees and small benches where some guardians were playing with their children. The scene blurred out and the background became filled with white light. A little boy ran towards me, with a model spaceship held high up on his right hand. He was shouting, "*I want to be a space explorer when I grow up. I will go to the stars!*" As he streaked past me, a little girl also appeared, running after him. She was holding something round that I did not see clearly, perhaps a model space city. She shouted in delight, "*I will build my own space city when I grow up.*"

I opened my eyes, feeling instant relief as my burden evaporated and my doubts disappeared. Tears poured down my face. I knew what I would like to achieve with my life. Over the next few months, I had a few similar experiences. I saw my death, clusters of space cities, the obsolesce of money and a new political structure unthinkable today. I saw fully immersive virtual reality fulfilling all desires as it provided experiential education and entertainment. I saw Planet Earth restored to its full glory as a Natural Reserve. I saw that Humanity has created a New Heaven and put an end to all conflict and suffering. Then suddenly, these experiences stopped completely.

After my taste of sweet Heaven, for years I had a major problem accepting that I am still living on planet Earth. I could not accept that we still need to work to make a living, that there is still war, disease and poverty. I could not accept that the world is so technologically primitive, still reliant on money and still so ugly. I was also unsure what other people would think of my experiences, so for years I did not share it with most people.

I read about psychology before and I knew how suggestible the human mind is. I knew that we could easily create false memories or hallucinations and experience them as real. Still, even if I had seen nothing but illusions, they are useful and beneficial illusions. They gave me the strength to break the limits of autism. They may also potentially inspire people to create a positive future for Humanity. I intend to share more of what I experienced with the world by writing another book.

C16: INNER HEALING

If there is one thing that the world needs right now more than anything else, I say that it is forgiveness. If there is one thing that the autism community needs more than anything else, I will also say that it is forgiveness. It is easy to create misunderstandings, conflict and hostility if you are autistic. Likewise, it is easy for people to bully, trick or torment you if you are autistic. When the autistic children grow up and start understanding what is happening to them, they become angry.

> *"Why must we always conform to and compromise with other people? We have rights too! People also ought to conform to us! Why are we being discriminated and despised? Why don't people accept us?"*

After becoming angry, they may set their anger on the world, as some do on the Internet today. Because many people do not listen to them or take them seriously, this hurts them and drives them to express increasingly radical views. Here is a paraphrase of some of the thoughts that I have encountered:

> *"We are the superior ones. We are the clever ones. We are the better people. We can do many things that the non-autistics cannot do. Unlike them, we are immune to irrational thinking. Unlike them, we do not conform to social brainwashing. Other people ought to listen to us. Why do they insist on curing us? Why do they insist on thinking that autism is a disease? Why do they invent things like genetic tests to screen out autistic babies? Stop discriminating against us! We are a race and culture equal if not superior to the non-autistics. We don't need your pity! Stop trying to destroy who we are!"*

It is already difficult enough to rear autistic children, but the parents of autistics also receive discrimination and unkind words from the people around them. It is understandable if some of them may feel upset or impatient with their autistic child. We are only human, after all.

The healing of our inner wounds can only start with forgiveness. My journey to leave the limits of autism is also a journey of learning to forgive. Firstly, I must forgive myself for being so stupid, awkward and slow. After that, I must forgive those people who had ridiculed, bullied and tormented me. Lastly, I must forgive the Divine for setting me on this planet of suffering. Only after I cleared all these stages can I see how I have contributed to my own suffering. This opens the way for me to change my perception and to accept love and concern from the people around me.

In some ways, I wrote this book as a tribute to forgiveness. It is not easy to write it because I have a commitment to mean what I write. If I do not write in this way, I would betray my inner integrity. This is why if I am unable to forgive someone, I chose not to pretend to or force myself to forgive because it is the "right" thing to do. I only forgive when I am ready to forgive. The same goes for gratitude and other emotions that I am "supposed" to feel. I know that some people may judge me harshly for being "emotionally immature" or unappreciative, but I prefer to answer to my inner conscience than to pretend to be who I am not.

I am now at an important stage of my life where I needed to let go and dive more deeply into the human experience to understand people. My parents, my teachers and friends as well as those who chose to ignore my work in Singapore, those who bullied me, those who cheated me etc. all came into my life to teach me forgiveness. Therefore, I am using this book as a platform for me to heal myself.

Emotional Problems

Traditionally, emotions were my weak spot, something that my logical mind could not tame or understand. Tackling emotions was like taking on a raging bull by its horns. When I started becoming aware of it, I was frightened and worried about this creature that felt so alien and unpredictable. Yet, in order to heal my inner wounds, I must also handle the secondary emotional problems that autism has created within me. I must confront my inner demons and worst nightmares in order to release the burden of autism.

Confusion & Shock

Everything was a maze that made no sense. Before I could react, everything has happened already. I was rushed, rushed and rushed all the time to catch up with the world around me. I did not know what to do, but people just wanted me to "do it". I did my best, but people still scolded me for making stupid mistakes or being slow. How might I know that I am not supposed to say this? How might I know that I must do this? How might I know this or that which everyone claimed is merely common sense? How could I do things that I cannot possibly follow? Please, have mercy on me. Please, do not torment me.

Despair
I lived in a world devoid of warmth, absent of social touch. No touch could comfort me; no love could reach me. Even when my mother sat beside me, I was oblivious to her love and concern. When people touched me, instead of feeling comfort and joy, I felt repulsed by the strange crawly feeling on my skin. When I tasted food, I could not appreciate the aromas.

Given free time, I found myself becoming even more anxious trying to find ways to occupy my time. While my friends and classmates enjoyed a great time together, I avoided the noise and distraction, trying desperately to read my book in a corner. Unable to understand meaning and intentions, my thoughts were incoherent and chaotic. No one could hear my voice, nor do I have a voice that expressed what was happening to me. I spoke facts and logic that had nothing to do with what I feel or who I am.

Frustration
I was stuck with people who refuse to listen to me, even though I was clearly right and they wrong. I knew how to do this school project perfectly, but they would rather force me to do it in their ineffective and inefficient way. I was only trying to focus, but many people would insist on interrupting and disturbing me.

Everything was supposed to work, according to logic. However, unexpected things happen. People refused to cooperate and spoiled my carefully thought out plans. No matter how many backups and contingencies I thought of, nothing worked. I wished I could do everything myself, yet I was confined to this pathetic human body so in need of rest, food and other troublesome tasks. I was confined to this slow human mind, so limited in its processing and learning powers that I can only read a textbook a day at most. Human limitations were too much for me to handle. I wanted to go back to where I came from, wherever that is.

Resentment
Why must I always conform to others? What about other people conforming to me? Why must they always set the rules? Why not let me set the rules for a change? What gives them the right to force me to conform? How can they insist that I should obey some irrational rules or perform unnecessary tasks without explanation or reason? They demand so many things of me that I was not capable of doing, yet when I told them what I wanted, the refused to give that to me.

Loneliness
Why do people turn against me for no reason? I was merely only trying to argue logically about the situation. Why must they insist on insulting me? Why must they bully me? Why must they do so such terrible things to me, who only came in goodwill to make the world a better place? They hated me. When I tried to show them what they were doing to me by using the same words and same expressions, they hated me even more. No one seemed to want to side with me, to give me comfort, to hear what I wanted to share. It was futile for me to do anything: Earthlings were simply too stubborn, too irrational, too strange.

Depression
I gave up. I could not do anything. No one will listen to me anyway. I just have to keep to myself and protect my own space as much as possible. A few times during my teenage years, I woke up deep at night and cried for no reason. I did not even sob; my tears simply flowed uncontrollably. Deep within me a little child wept, "*No one loves me. No one accepts me. No one hears me. Why am I still here? I want to go home.*" Yet, I could not even hear myself. Most parts of me just wondered why tears were flowing so freely. "*How irritating to have to wake up and then unable to sleep again for a few hours,*" they thought.

About Emotional Healing

I believe that within each of us exists a storehouse or library of all kinds of sentient beings, each with different agendas. [This may show up in an obvious manner for people with split personalities.] These different parts of us often quarrel with each other, creating unending internal confusion within us. When we do emotional healing work, we act as the diplomat cum politician for our Inner Kingdom. We enter into the chaotic Parliament, hear the voices of each faction and then seek to find a resolution to create a win-win situation for everyone.

In this way, we facilitate the work of all the people within us, focus their unified efforts to create useful and positive work and then bring them to a grander and larger expression of themselves. As we lead our own kingdom to unity, meaning and freedom, we lead ourselves along the same journey too.

Imagine, for instance, a dictatorial government fond of broadcasting the official beliefs that every citizen should have. When it makes decisions, it does not care about what impact it will have on the citizens, trampling on their rights whenever it sees fit. To ensure conformity, many spies roamed the country. If these spies hear of anyone who dares to disagree with the official policy or beliefs, they catch these "disloyal traitors" and dump them in a concentration camp. The frightened citizens are resigned to spread the propaganda, praising it endlessly.

Some of the citizens who have suffered grave injustice can no longer stand by and do nothing. They become resistance fighters, sabotaging the government forces so that it will pay attention to their plight. Instead of listening to their voice and seeking to find peace with them, the government responds with overwhelming military force, cracking down on the resistance and slaughtering innocent suspects. The more paranoid the government becomes, the more it alienates the people. The resistance grows in power, until one day, it manages to topple the government. However, it does so at the cost of horrendous casualties on both sides. In the resulting power vacuum, the country falls into total chaos. The surviving citizens run amok, rioting, looting and raping freely.

Many of us today have the privilege to speak our minds freely, and can no longer imagine living under an oppressive government. Yet we often run our inner world like a dictator, refusing to listen to the voices of our people. Anyone dares disagree? "*Make them agree!*" Anyone dares to stop us? "*Silence them!*" No matter what form of emotional healing we do, when we deny something, we are putting it there. What resists, persists. (e.g. Don't think of a pink elephant.)

It is useless to only partially forgive a person and try to bury or destroy those parts that refuse to forgive. It is useless to deny what we know is the truth, for only the truth will set us free. Therefore, when we find hatred, lust, greed or any other negative emotions within us, we must first accept them as our inner truth before we let go of them. Think about the unhappy citizens within us who have grievances to redress. They only become radical terrorists because we are not willing to listen to them. To heal ourselves, we must undertake the journey to be the Savior of our Inner Kingdom.

Emotional Releasing

Emotional Releasing is a tool that has helped me. Not all people benefit from it, so I believe that the effectiveness of this work depends on the intuitive abilities of the facilitator and the emotional readiness of client. Ideally, the client:

1. Is ready to change his life
2. Practices inner honesty
3. Speaks in unison with all of his inner selves
4. Is willing to make the commitment for change

Theory

To me, emotional releasing is a four-step process of:

1. Exploring our emotions
2. Understanding the origin of our emotions
3. Releasing the old emotional programming
4. Creating new emotional programming

The first 2 steps help us become aware of our emotional situation so that we can understand its nature and see if it serves us. If it does not serve us, then we can choose to let go of it and choose a replacement that serves us. My facilitators liken the packages of emotions and beliefs in our mind to programs installed on our computer hard drive. Emotionally troubled people have some viruses or bad software on their computer hard drive, causing their computer to malfunction. The emotional releasing process is like pressing the delete button on the computer keyboard to remove such bad software.

How it works (for my case)

Two facilitators, a married couple, guided me during the 2 to 3 hour session. I rested on a comfortable mattress on the floor, while they broadcasted smooth, calming music from a CD player. They started by counting me down from a highly awake state to a state of inner awareness. When they have finished, they say something to this effect: "*Intend for your subconscious to show you what you are ready to release today*". After that, I paid attention to and reported on any inner thoughts and emotions. I usually see a picture immediately that expanded into a story as I described it. [Other people may take many minutes of prodding to begin sensing anything.]

The stories I saw may be from my childhood memory or it may be something I did not recall experiencing at all. The facilitators asked me to pinpoint the time (roughly the number of years) the story occurred as soon as I lock on one of them. My facilitators never questioned the stories, no matter how exotic. However, I took these with a pinch of salt because I knew about the suggestibility of the human mind. I believed that my subconscious uses such stories to communicate, not necessarily to recall events. So rather than judge if the story was real or not, I paid attention to how it related to my existing life situation.

When I made an emotional breakthrough with the story, I would feel an extraordinary sensation in my whole body. Intense emotions would arise from my body and I may shout, cry, hit the pillow nearby, get into an involuntary spasm etc. For some people, this outburst may last for an hour. I considered this the highlight of the releasing process, and the most fulfilling part of being a facilitator.

After the initial outburst, the facilitators supplied me with some releasing statements and affirmations. I felt the meaning of these statements, connected with all the different parts of me and affirmed these statements in unison. If these statements hit the mark, even more emotions emerged from me. The process continued until I felt emotionally tired and empty. A great sense of relief, lightness and joy then filled me, much like a beautiful landscape after a storm. This sensation may last anywhere from a few days to a few weeks.

Choosing Releasing Statements
We can choose among millions of possible statements. The role of the facilitator is to help the client pick suitable statements, although it is theoretically possible for the client to do the same for himself. Relying mostly on intuition and experience, my facilitators did not have a systematic way of picking the statements. This is similar to my style. When I played the role of the facilitator (privately for friends or while participating in workshops), I may see certain images or feel an urge to say certain words.

In order to explain the process to other people, I came up with my own theory and explanation on emotional releasing. To construct the package, I build:
1. A set of Releasing Statements (R)
2. Followed by a set of Corresponding Affirmations (A)
3. And finally, Affirmation Seals (S)
4. Sometimes, we will also use Easing Statements (E) to remove the resistance to uttering the statements

Releasing Example 1
R1: I release hating myself for all the weaknesses and failures that I have.
R2: I release being overcritical and judgmental of myself.

E1: I allow myself to see that what happened is not my fault.
E2: I allow myself to see that I have done the best that I could, and there is nothing more I could have done in that situation.
E3: I allow myself to see my own perfection and beauty.
E4: I allow myself to forgive myself.

A1: I forgive myself right now, right here.
E5: I allow myself to love myself.

A2: I choose to love and accept myself the way I AM now.
A3: And I open myself to see that love, joy and peace is my "True Self".

R1: I choose to let go of all my self-judgment and hatred forever.
S1: And so it is.

Releasing Example 2
R1: I release my fear of failing in my relationship with my partner.
R2: I release my fear to be hurt again, as I was in the past.
E1: I allow myself to see that I am safe.
E2: I allow myself to see that no one can hurt or destroy me.

R3: I release all decisions to close my heart out of fear of being hurt.
E3: And I allow myself to open my heart to my partner.
S1: So it is.
A1: I choose now to open my heart to love and to receive love.
S2: So it is.

R4: I release my fear of being controlled and overpowered by my partner.
S3: And so it is.
R5: I release the need to punish my partner for what she has done to me.
S4: And so it is.
R6: I release all decisions never to forgive my partner.
S5: And so it is.
A2: I choose to forgive my partner unconditionally; right here, right now.
S6: And so it is.

R7: I release to look at my partner through eyes of the past.
E4: I allow myself to see new positive possibilities for our relationship.
R8: I release my fear of being misunderstood and rejected if I speak my Inner Truth.
S7: And so it is.

A3: I choose now to speak my Truth and express all my feelings freely.
S8: And so it is.

More examples - *http://www.ireleasenow.com/Ireleasenow.htm*

Disclaimer

I am unsure of the effects of emotional releasing on other autistics and aware that only some people have benefited from it. Hence, I could not recommend it for autism treatment. I believe that emotional releasing is not a cure for emotional problems, but a tool to facilitate the changes already happening within us. Please consult a qualified professional for advice on autism treatment.

My inner policy

1. **Let the Future Remain Open**: What happens in the past is true for the past. However, the past must stay in its place. If we let our past restrict our future, history will repeat itself again.

2. **Beliefs are not Absolute**: I believe in my truth, but allow myself to change what I believe in. I do not say that because something is not my truth, consistent with my actions or in line with my policy, that I disallow myself from considering it. If I kept the same policies and beliefs, I will not be able to accomplish what I have done today.

3. **Truth is also Functional**: Our world does not fit into only one definition, perspective or standard. As there are many possible truths, I choose the truth that allows me to express myself more fully in this world.

4. **Do not force emotions**: I do not allow moral and cultural conventions such the thought that I should feel grateful for help to force myself to feel differently from what I really feel.

5. **Do not force beliefs**: I do not change my beliefs to suit social norms. I change them only when have investigated enough to understand the situation.

6. **Give unto the world what we need**: If I need love, I give love away. If I need knowledge, I share what I know with others. If I need wealth, I help others become wealthy. This helps me to realize that I have what I lack all along.

7. **Allow authority, not control**: There are two kinds of teachers in the world: those who teach us what to do, and those who teach us what *not* to do. I respect both of them for their roles but do not allow them to control me.

C17: ACCEPTING MYSELF

Planet Earth is a place of severe limitations. For every choice we make, we sacrifice countless other possibilities. Our actions may take years, if not decades, to bear fruit. Because of these limitations, it is important to plan our goals carefully and then commit thoroughly to them. Years may pass before we obtain feedback on our plans, making it hard to change course. In the midst of such imperfection, sacrifice and struggle, how do we accept Planet Earth? In the midst of facing discrimination, deceit and bad behavior, how do we accept Humanity?

I believe that the answer lies with accepting my self. I am part of the world, merely a smaller version of it. I embody its principles and work according to its laws. The bad things I dislike about this world also exist within me. If I cannot see the good things about this world, that is because I do not see them within me. Hence, I set forth on a journey to believe in myself, so that I can believe in the world around me. I read inspiring material, reflected on them and then used emotional releasing to open myself to the 5 core beliefs.

The 5 Core Beliefs

I am inherently good
- I release the idea that I am bad, defective or evil.
- I release my fear of my dark side.
- I allow myself to see that I am inherently good and pure.
- I allow myself to trust and to believe myself.
- I release all my decisions never to forgive myself.
- I allow myself to stop punishing myself for my mistakes and failures.
- I release all the anger and hatred against myself.
- I choose to forgive myself unconditionally.

I am beautiful
- I release the idea that I am a cosmic mistake unworthy of respect or dignity.
- I release the idea that I can never redeem my imperfections or myself.

- I release my disgust and rejection of my human body.
- I release the idea that my body is imperfect and inadequate.
- I allow myself to love and treasure my body.
- I accept my body.
- I allow myself to be born into my body.
- I release the idea that I am weak, incapable or inadequate.
- I allow myself to see my strengths, talents and contributions.
- I allow myself to see my own beauty and magnificence.
- I release the fear that I must always win or do better than other people in order to prove myself.
- I allow myself to stop comparing myself with other people.
- I release my fear of accepting my greatness.
- I allow myself to accept my own beauty and goodness.
- I allow myself to love myself as who I am.

My existence is meaningful
- I release my fear of being trapped on Planet Earth.
- I release my fear of the dark side.
- I release my fear of being overwhelmed by the world around me.
- I allow myself to take control of my life.
- I release my fear that there is no meaning in life.
- I release my fear that I am alone, and no one will help me.
- I allow myself to trust in the Higher Power Beyond, knowing that I will be safe and protected.
- I allow myself to accept and love my life.

My life is perfect
- I release myself from the judgment and criticism of others.
- I release myself from the limiting labels and opinions placed on me by others.
- I release my fear of being overpowered by the people around me.
- I release any decisions to give my power away.
- I allow myself to take back all my power now.
- I release my fear of failure and of losing all my achievements.
- I release the fear that others would judge and criticize me if I allow myself to be who I really am.
- I allow myself to change my life in order to express who I really am.
- I release the idea that I cannot grow beyond my limitations.

- I allow myself to live my full potential and express my full abilities now.

I am the World
- I release my fear that other people will misunderstand and reject me if I speak my Truth and express my feelings.
- I release my fear of speaking my Truth.
- I release my fear of expressing my feelings.
- I release my anger and hatred for those who do not agree with my truth.
- I release my desire to force my truth on others.
- I release the idea that I am always right.
- I release the idea that my way is the best and only way.
- I release my need to convince others of my truth and my beliefs.
- I open myself now to respect the truth of others and their beliefs.
- I release all decisions never to forgive other people for the wrongs and misunderstandings they committed in the past.
- I release my fear that I would fail in my relationship with other people.
- I release my fear of taking responsibility for my part in the relationship.
- I released looking at other people through eyes of the past.
- I allow myself to accept the people around me.
- I allow myself to accept my personal situation.

My Subconscious Story

Almost all of us are living a story about Who We Are, how we have arrived at our present situation and how we wish to live in the future. This story creates our personal history, allowing us to find meaning in our lives. However, like a bonsai gardener, it also stops us from growing outside our limited definition of Who We Are today into Who We Could Be tomorrow.

I used to have a story about myself being a talented genius who had much to contribute to the world. Unfortunately, other people were too narrow-minded or stupid to notice my genius. My life was about struggling to gain the recognition and respect that was my birthright. Although I wanted to implement a brilliant idea or project, but I could never find the right people, resources, connection or guidance to do it. No one ever gave me the chance to share my genius and contribution with the entire world.

While writing a play in 2005, I created a character to express my subconscious archetype: He is a handsome man who knows all about the magical arts. Alone by himself, he moves like the wind, roaming the world to help the weak and needy. A firm believer of peace, he does not fight unless he has no choice. When he draws his sword, lighting erupts from the sky. Without moving his body or uttering a word, the sheer presence of his sword strikes down all villains. Then he declares, "*I am a genius of the first class. Heaven and Earth trembles before me.*"

My story ran my life without challenge until my disastrous business failure. With it, I realized just how arrogant I was. It was indeed true that I had much general knowledge, creativity and a deep understanding of spirituality. I had made certain achievements such as publishing my book almost single-handedly. I had many skills such as English writing, business, graphics design, photography, computer programming and computer repair. It seemed that I would have no problems finding a job if I wanted to find one.

I was ignorant of my failings. I did not realize that I did not have respect and empathy for others. I did not know how to sell my talents for the practical use by other people. I did not have the practical sense and understanding of the real life situations so my work was of limited help to the world. Even worse, I was too impatient in trying to start a business with unsuitable and inexperienced people to escape my mother's nagging that I find a job immediately.

My arrogance put off some potential employers, partners and friends. It has probably contributed to my lack of success in Singapore. Hence, before I came to Macau, I committed to humility and empathy. I committed to accepting other people as who they are instead of requiring them to meet me at my level. I reworked my autism presentation and to convey useful information that was emotionally inspiring. As a result, I witnessed parents crying during my sharing. I have finally found recognition and acceptance.

I learnt that I could not let my story run my life. When things happened to me, I used to relate to my story (e.g. consoling myself that other people were too stupid). When I responded to different situations, I would react from my story (e.g. being arrogant because I thought I was a genius). I realized that every time I felt hurt, upset or disappointed in something that other people have done or not done, I was living from my story. Every time I expected or required something from myself or other people, I was getting into my story. Every time I hurt others in order to punish them, I was living my story. It is not easy to step out of my story – I am still living part of it even today. However, I do my best.

Questions that helped me leave my story

- Does this situation remind me of anything from my past? What if I decide to disregard what happened to me and choose freely again? What would I choose?
- Am I following my calling if I make this choice? Am I serving the world / God / sentient beings if I make this choice?
- If this (event) happens, what is the worst that will happen to me? Can I live with that?
- How do I make the situation whole again? How do I use the situation as if it is already perfect?
- What is the solution that will make the problem irrelevant?

A test to check my emotional healing

- If I am constantly feeling negative, then I am not healed.
- If I judge people as inferior or superior to me, then I am not healed. The unwanted traits of these people are what I need to heal in myself.
- If I seek to control others or let others control me, then I am not healed.
- If there is a single disagreeing thought in my mind, then I am not healed. Quashing thoughts though mental techniques or fatigue does not count.
- If there is a single emotion in me that I reject, then I am not healed.
- If I could not feel meaning in my life, then I am not healed.

C18: A QUICK REVIEW OF MY JOURNEY

My journey on Planet Earth was a series of unending struggles to adapt. I was lonely and could never make friends because I did not understand relationships, different perspectives, intention and emotions. I was clumsy because the world was like a flat photograph to me and I did not know that I had a body. Tying neat shoelaces was nearly impossible for me.

My world was in constant confusion, anxiety and suffering without enjoyable sensory experiences and social intimacy to give relief. Nothing I planned went right because I lacked the ability to plan and intuitively "sense my future". Other people saw me as a quiet and nerdy boy. No one suspected that I had a unique neurological disability. Society did not exempt me from social rules: I had to study in class like everyone else.

Today, I can look at people in the eye. Today, I can play with children and give them hugs. Today, I can understand the implications of my choices and make practical decisions. Today, I have many genuine friends from many backgrounds, whom I love and whom love me. And I have a dream...

Tomorrow, I shall reconcile with my mother. Tomorrow, I shall become financially independent so that I can do what I like. Tomorrow, we shall create a future for Humanity together without war, disease, poverty and suffering. After stepping beyond the limits of autism, my journey to change the world has only just begun.

My Inner Commitments

My 1st Time Committing
When I read the Self Improvement book in 1997 (when I was in Secondary 3), I realize that I exist, and am separate from other people. With this new sense of self, I broke away from my traditional of merely storing and processing data.

With my very own Inner World, I now have the power to imagine new possibilities for myself. The problem was that now I have to choose what to do with this power. At that moment, I was not ready to focus this power and use it at its maximum potential. Hence, I made 3 commitments that would make me an Eternal Student:

1. *I will learn more about myself and how my mind works*
2. *I will improve myself constantly to prepare for new challenges*
3. *I will express myself and declare my choices and creativity to the world*

That was a good start but it could not bring me far. I know a (suspected) autistic friend who became an Eternal Student. Refusing to take a job, he reads books, joins many workshops, tries new experiences and networks with many people. He was lucky enough to have parents who can afford to allow him to do that. Not me.

My 2nd Time

With my own effort, I learnt about many subjects like psychology, science, politics, history and religion, Soon, I concluded that the Planet Earth had too many major problems like war, disease and poverty. I decided to fix these problems. Hence, around 1998, I made an additional commitment: "*I will get very rich, use the money to create a global research institution and employ the best scientists to devise ways to solve all the world's problems*". I declared my Life Mission according to my understanding at that time.

To the people around me, that was a ridiculous goal. Nevertheless, it gave me something to aim for so that I can find meaning in my life. I added financial education and business law to my personal syllabus and doubled my effort. Despite all the discouragement and skepticism I hear, I focused on Positive Thinking and took for granted my ability to achieve my goal. However, if I went on without awareness of my disability, I would fail.

My 3rd Time

In 2001, I discovered autism and received a diagnosis. That event led me to make another commitment: "*I will accept Who I Am, and be proud of it*". I overdid this commitment. My self-esteem went from being a downtrodden carpet to a hot-air balloon high above the sky. My thoughts and actions carried the message, "I am better than you!" Living like this for years, I would have stopped my growth if I did not have the opportunity to commit to another very important commitment.

My 4th Time

In mid-2002, a friend introduced me to the works of Neale Donald Walsch. The controversy surrounding his work did not interest me, but the philosophy he mentioned did. His work reassured me that our world does have meaning, that life is not a competition against the world or other people, and that people have innately love but they have forgotten their goodness. After I read the first few books, everything fit together in my mind. With this, I made a crucial commitment: "*I commit to trust and accept Planet Earth and its inhabitants.*"

This commitment also meant that I will work on my hidden emotional issues, and that I will meet Earthlings at their level instead of demanding that they meet me at mine. Emotional Releasing and other emotional healing work was just what I need. Over the next few years, my emotions rapidly awakened and I felt rage, desire, warmth and a sense of well-being. I went through an emotional roller coaster as I integrated my emotions. The people around me did not understand what was happening. No one could offer me any advice or tell me what was going on inside of me. Instead, some were disturbed that I displayed strong yet immature emotions and developed the ability to lie. In the absence of external guidance, I handled most of my changes alone.

My 5th Time

After I published "Mirror Mind" in November 2005, I tried in vain to get people to recognize my work and become financially independent through it. My immature attitude coupled with the lack of experience and mentors meant that I had limited success and many serious setbacks. I learnt that I did not have all the answers I thought that I had. I had to stop being arrogant.

Things changed when I came to Macau in October 2006. I witnessed for the first time parents moved to tears by my sharing. I learnt about charity and compassion as well as the power of touch and eye contact with some of my new friends. By now, most of the emotional storms have stopped. My emotions became tamer and I felt more certain, stable and ready to engage with the world around me. This came together in my new commitments:

1. *To work from my heart*
2. *To honor and respect the inner truth of everyone, including myself*

My 6th Time

I realized that I needed to change my sharing from just talking about autism to sharing something that the parents and teachers can apply. My sponsor suggested that a free autism booklet would help, so I made one. In order to encourage me to become independent, my sponsor stopped organizing events for me. I had to rely on my own connections and efforts to promote my work. Thus, I sharpened my focus and asked those who invited me to choose the topics for sharing rather than just speaking on what I liked. Realizing that people in the region understood Mandarin more than English, I also decided to speak the language that I used to dislike intensely. This book is a result of this new understanding, and my commitment to:

1. *Serve the world according to my inspiration*
2. *Express myself in a way that people can most easily understand*

My 7th Time

After many attempts where I tried but failed to earn a living from my autism work, my mother could no longer tolerate my lack of financial security. When she confronted me emotionally, I decided to stop my autism work and obtain full-time employment. With this, I committed to:

1. *Letting go of my over attachment to my ideals*
2. *Experiencing the life of typical Earthlings in order to understand them more deeply*

What happened

1. **Mental Separation** – This separated the verbal, intelligent part of my mind from the non-verbal part. It allowed me to build up my thinking capacity and language skills.

2. **Conscious Will** – This created the boundary between me and other people, creating the "self". It also woke me up to self-consciousness at the same time.

3. **Creativity** – This activated my problem solving ability and allowed me to solve many problems that I did not know of. It also trained me to look at problems using different perspectives and to accept change with a positive attitude.

4. **Direction** – This creates the Initial Motivation to take control of my life and focus my lifestyle so that I can achieve my goal.

5. **Autism Awareness** – This allowed me to realize my differences from other people and to accept myself. It also helped me understand other people by knowing the ways they are different from me,

6. **Worldly Trust** – When I have faith and trust in myself, I begin to trust in the world and see the new opportunities to live meaningfully.

7. **Purpose** –Someone has to convince me to take the great leap to connect with Humanity, like a salesperson pitching: "*Live this life, because it is so wonderful and exciting!*" Once convinced, I committed wholeheartedly.

8. **Emotional Awareness** – Without dealing with my hidden emotional problems, I could not move on to create a new life for myself.

9. **Relationships** – I had to develop a working understanding of relationships before I can continue in my social development. By observation of both my environment and slowly awakening social instincts, I am able to deduce this concept, apply it, learn from experience and calibrate my future responses.

10. **Humility** – I had to let go of the excessive confidence from my past so that I can connect with other people and accept my role as an equal or subordinate.

11. **Service** – I realized that I derive the most meaning and joy by serving the world. Thus, I chose to live a life of service.

12. **Practicality** – I had to pay attention to the situation that other people encounter, integrate advice from experienced people and combine my own perspective and ideas so that my work is both original and useful.

C19: CONSCIOUS INTERVENTION

I propose the idea that the experience of autism arises from a distorted self-awareness. Our self-awareness guides our thoughts and behavior. It also allows us to infer the same process happening to other people (e.g. socialization). However, we can only act on and change what we can see. When blurring or distortions interrupt this feedback, we experience many syndromes of autism such as poor executive planning and low empathy.

Using the metaphor of a mirror to represent self-awareness, we all have varying distortions in our mirror (e.g. we may think we are smarter or stupider than we are). However, the autistic's mirror has distortions so severe that it breaks his self-awareness into confusing disconnected fragments. For instance, he may not consider his body as part of himself. As a result, he experiences life like watching television from a perspective outside his body.

With distortions in his perception of time and emotions, the autistic can easily underestimate the effort and commitment required to accomplish things. I liken this to TV programmes, where producers routinely compress time and remove mundane experiences for the viewer's enjoyment. In 20 minutes, we can see Albert Einstein grow up, discover the Theory of Relativity and receive international acclaim. We saw faded photographs instead of experiencing his life moment by moment with him. We heard commentaries instead of feeling his actual fears, aspirations and beliefs. Unpleasant experiences lasting many years may end up in one mere sentence. This made his painful and difficult accomplishments sound so easy, fast and effortless. Experiencing life like an endless TV programme, how can we fault the autistic for being over-confident of his abilities and rigidly persistent of his goals?

I do not believe that autism arises due to insufficient practice with social skills. I do not believe that we can eliminate autism if we dumb down social skills into simple stories and spoon-feed these via behavior therapy to autistic children. I believe that when autistics develop a coherent self-awareness, they will develop the capacity for empathy and relating automatically.

My Key Assumptions

1. I can generalize the experiences I had to similar self-conscious high functioning autistics.
2. The criterion for adapting to Planet Earth is if the autistic finds joy, meaning and acceptance of Earthly Life. The absence of inappropriate behavior does not provide a true conclusion.
3. The negative experiences created by being ill equipped for Planet Earth make autistics fearful of life. We must convince them to trust and accept this world before they are willing to receive help.
4. Only our innate instincts allow us to handle Life. Memorizing social rules is a tiring chore that does not create the unconscious competency allowing autistics to enjoy the human experience.
5. Such innate instincts will activate themselves if not for certain obstructions. Once we remove them, the human brain has many fail-safes and can recover from most problems.
6. Many of the obstacles are psychological in nature. With the right understanding and tools, we can guide the self-aware autistic to do Inner Work to resolve the obstacles.
7. As each group of instincts activate, they require appropriate real-life experiences and sufficient time to mature fully.
8. However, during the maturation process, the autistic may experience great stresses due to "developmental compression" – growth and maturation processes usually taking years may happen in a few months. He may seem to digress or become unpredictable as he tries to adapt to his new experiences.
9. As the instincts are self-correcting, guidance and patience may be sufficient by themselves. Therapy may be required only for secondary issues like biological toxins or psychological disorders.

Stages of Conscious Intervention

1. **Persuasion => Seeing Big Picture => Trust** – The autistic is like a tourist who is considering whether to visit Planet Earth. Someone from the "tour agency" has to convince him that Planet Earth is a good, exciting and meaningful place. Once he can trust the world, he can heal his emotional wounds and open himself to new experiences for his instincts to activate.

2. **Emotional Healing => Emotional Awareness** – Autistics have secondary emotional issues such as emotional scars from being bullied and paralyzing anxiety due to self-doubt. As they are resolved, they develop awareness of their emotional processes and state. This sets the foundation for the activation and discovery of his instincts.
3. **Real Life Practice => Application** – To help his instincts mature, it is best if he can observe and practice social skills in a safe yet socially realistic place with people who understand his difficulties.
4. **Challenge => Achievement** – When he is ready, it is best to co-create certain challenges with him that is appropriate for his level of understanding, takes into account his preferences and is of a practical nature. He will gain confidence and experience, resulting in eventual achievement.

Encountering the Human Instincts

1. **Consciousness**: The autistic develops his capacity to become aware of and to reflect on his life. This lays the foundation for Conscious Intervention.
2. **Will**: The autistic discovers his individuality, even if it is in a limited form. Other than acting from reaction or obedience, he can also choose consciously. This makes Conscious Intervention possible.
3. **Emotions**: Emotional healing helps the autistic become sensitive to his emotions and his hidden emotional issues. Resolving these empowers him to own his emotions, history and environment. He can then choose new ways of responding to the situation.
4. **Relationships**: Emotions bring forth a hidden dimension to relationships that go beyond the transactional. In a safe social environment without emotional issues blocking him, his relating instincts can then unfold.
5. **Body**: Emotional healing also helps the autistic to own his body and sensory experiences. This sets the stage for developing bodily awareness, which activates the Physics Instinct.
6. **Experience** – Accepting his mind, emotions, body and environment, it is only a matter of time before he understands the human experience and adapts successfully to Planet Earth.

Building Trust

We can build trust with works that are:

1. **Inspiring**: They present the goodness, beauty and meaning of Life, creating strong, positive feelings in us.
2. **Logical**: They make logical sense and are not purely social-emotional.
3. **Spiritual**: They go deeper than typical self-improvement work to explore the big picture of Life.

I believe that certain philosophical, religious and mystical works may be of help. I have positive experiences with Zen Buddhism and the "Conversations with God" series by Neale Donald Walsch.

Emotional Awareness

I believe that self-conscious autistics have different developmental needs. Instead of emotions laying a meaningful foundation for their intellect to grow, their intellect lays the logical foundation of trust for their emotions to develop. After developing building trust, these emotional exploration methods may help:

Emotional Healing Work: The books that I recommend include "You can change your life" by Tim Laurence and "The Journey" by Brandon Bays. I do not recommend using "Neuro-Linguistic Programming" (NLP) or the "Emotional Freedom Technique" (EFT) for this purpose. I believe that these do not promote conscious emotional exploration that would foster emotional awareness.

Writing Stories & Scripts: Writing allows our subconscious to express our desires and inner state. We can also explore the experience of what it is like to be human. I believe that this can be a very powerful tool even if the work produced is not of publishable quality.

Drama & Performances: We can act out what we write. I could close my eyes and imagine myself on stage with other actors. This way, I can act out my own script the way I like without incurring much expense and effort. I know of a form of emotional healing work named "psychodrama" where people act out their emotional issues with each other. However, I am not comfortable with its system of turn taking and requirement of interacting with other people.

Possible Adventures

We can do many projects in Life. There are so many things that we can do that we are often overwhelmed with choices. Generally, I focus on work that has three components:

1. **Meaningful**: We feel that our work goes beyond mere survival.
2. **Useful**: The work benefits other people and us.
3. **Helpful**: We create the greatest impact with the least effort and time.
4. **Socially Acceptable**: The work is of a form accepted by society.

My own examples

Write / Paint / Create: If we have something to share that can serve the world, we can write them down or draw them out. Even if they cannot allow one to make a living from them, or they can still be a good hobby.

Start a business: We can take a job to gain some experience, then try simple businesses like trade fair booths to understand how things work. I recommend that we consider such experiments as real life education: realistic enough to learn from but small enough to minimize possible losses. In time to come, we can progress to more complex business projects. These usually require experienced and able partners or advisors to ensure their success.

Invent something: If we have a talent for invention, we can help better Humanity and maybe get rich too. Again, major inventions usually require experienced and able partners or advisors to ensure their success.

Participate in a political / religious cause: If we have something close to our hearts, we can join a cause. Seeing how other people put their ideals into action can help us learn a lot about life on Planet Earth.

Conclusion

Autistics have different developmental needs Until other people help to fulfill these needs, the autistics' growth becomes stunted and they remain at odds with the world.

People often require autistics to conform to social demands without respecting their psychological needs. Even if an autistic no longer has socially inappropriate behavior, he may still feel angry compromising with rules that do not make sense, depressed because he could never get his plans right and anxious with worrisome thoughts about the unpredictable tomorrow.

I believe that no one should live solely for the sake of other people, and this includes autistics. An autistic does not live for the sake of our social norms. An autistic does not live so that he can pretend to be normal. An autistic does not live so that he can be useful to society. I believe that like every one of us, an autistic can choose to live because he enjoys living. An autistic can choose to live because he cares for his family and friends. An autistic can choose to live because he is working to fulfill a great vision of the future. May we build a bridge of peace and meaning between autistics and non-autistics.

C20: THE FUTURE OF AUTISM

I see a future where we can change reality at will. I see a world where we can enter each other's realities and experience their inner world. We can dance on symbols and swim with music. We can enter fairy tales and become mythical characters. These are possible with fully immersive virtual reality and "mind-reading computers" decades away. In it, we can feel the soft wind blowing on our face, hold a glass of water and look at the beautiful clouds in the sky, without noticing that it is not real. We can create, manipulate and remove objects using our thought and sculpt a movie in a week by ourselves. Such technologies release us from our physical limitations, making most disabilities obsolete.

Imagine the autistic child exploring Platonic shapes in an imaginary world we can observe right in front of us. Imagine him becoming the mathematical equations that reveal the beauty of our universe. Imagine him traveling to distant worlds on his very own spaceship and meeting new alien cultures. Changing their shape and form, his parents and friends can become his favorite toys and abstract shapes. His teachers can become the story characters of his imagination to guide him on learning about the human condition. When he is ready, he can join the other children to learn about the world of his ancestors. He will become the ocean, the animals and the clouds. He will experience the lives of the people who came before him. Why read a story when you can become the characters? Why read a textbook when you can rediscover the insights and discoveries by yourself?

This future may owe a lot to autistics. The inner mental operating systems in the minds of the autistics may well be the design of our future computer interface. The research of how autistics develop consciousness and empathy may well pave the way for the sentient computer intelligences of tomorrow.

I believe that the problems of our world cannot be solved at the level at which they were created. To create new solutions to our old problems, we must look beyond our worldview and leave our comfort zone. I hope that there is room for the new perspectives and contributions of those without formal qualifications and accomplishments like myself.

C21: CONCLUSION

Autism work is not just about helping socially handicapped people to integrate into mainstream society. How we treat autistics is not merely a question for special education. The politics we see around us is our demonstration of our inner politics. The wars, uncertainty and fear we see around us is a reflection of the same processes within us. The same goes for the phenomena of autism and our policies concerning it. Closing the gap between the autistics and non-autistics is part of the story of how Humanity will learn to live with diversity and accept each other.

Planet Earth is a complicated place. On one hand, most of us still need to focus on survival. On the other hand, we need to find meaning to live fulfilling lives. Meaning goes beyond blending in, making friends, good grades, full-time jobs and marriage. How could we find meaning in the midst of survival? How could autistics find meaning with life on Planet Earth? I hope that my work will help inspire many people to create their own answers to these challenging questions.

C22: ACKNOWLEDGMENTS

I dedicate this book to my mother, who was instrumental in my growth and who still supported me despite her disagreement with me.

I thank Mum & Dad for their support, upbringing and great sacrifices.

This book would not be possible without the support, guidance and help I received in Hong Kong, Macau and China. I especially wish to thank Ms. Patricia, Mandu, Francis Yu, Dr. Lai, Ms. Ming, Rebecca, Kitty, Sonia, Marilyn and many other wonderful people. My experiences in these foreign lands opened my eyes to new social frontiers and provided me with many opportunities to mature.

I thank my friends in Singapore for their guidance and moral support, including Clara Lau, John Yeo, Anne Lim and Helen.

Lastly, I thank autism for showing me the grandness of the human experience by depriving me of it.

C23: PRAYER OF PRACTICALITY

Inner Inspiration
Remind me of why I came into this life
So that I may pray with sincerity

‹a moment of silence for reflection›

Inner Inspiration, lead me to practice my ideals
May I learn from those whom I dislike
May I appreciate criticism that insults me
May I learn the key to harmony from conflicts
May I demonstrate wisdom in times of error
May I remain clear when faced with my desires
May I honor this prayer when facing trouble
May I inspire those whom I find wanting
May I be wise enough to celebrate my suffering

Inner Inspiration, lead me to use myself as my instrument
To comfort others through comforting myself
To understand others through understanding myself
To love others through loving myself
And to become the change that I seek

For it is by self-experience that one is touched
By self-forgiving that one is forgiven
By moving with the world that one moves the world
And by making history that one understands history

Amen.

Written by Eric Chen
Inspired by the Prayer of Saint Francis
http://iautistic.com

C24: MY HISTORY TIME LINE

YEAR	:AGE:	WHAT HAPPENED
1982	: 00 :	I was born in December
1989	: 06 :	Primary 1 (mainstream school)
1990	: 07 :	Primary 2
1991	: 08 :	Primary 3
1992	: 09 :	Primary 4
1993	: 10 :	Primary 5
1994	: 11 :	Primary 6
1995	: 12 :	Secondary 1 (mainstream school)
1996	: 13 :	Secondary 2
1997	: 14 :	Secondary 3
1998	: 15 :	Secondary 4
1999	: 16 :	Polytechnic Year 1 (Diploma in Logistics Engineering & Management)
2000	: 17 :	Polytechnic Year 2 / Discovered Autism in an MSNBC article in December
2001	: 18 :	Polytechnic Year 3 / Diagnosed by the Autism Resource Centre (Singapore)
2002	: 19 :	Graduated from the Polytechnic / Drafted by the Singapore Army
2004	: 21 :	Completed Military Service
2005	: 22 :	Published "Mirror Mind", my first autism book / Volunteered to help 2 friends with their amateur theatre
2006	: 23 :	Failed to start a business with 2 friends in Singapore / Started my autism work in Macau, Hong Kong & China
2007	: 24 :	Published this book / Decided to stop autism work and find employment